THE FLAME OF GRACE

by

DONNA M. STONE

'For such a time as this'
Es 4:14

May God bless you with the
healing that awaits—

Donna M. Stone
2022

THE FLAME OF GRACE
© 2021 by Donna M. Stone All Rights Reserved

ISBN: 978 1-7376560-0-5

All Bible verse references in the book are taken from Wesley Study Bible; New Revised Standard Version. Nashville: Abingdon Press, 2009.

Contact the author at: theflameofgrace@gmail.com

Cover and interior design by Alane Pearce, Pearce Writing Services LLC
Editing by Alane Pearce, Pearce Professional Writing Services.
Contact: apearcewriting@gmail.com

Cover artwork is by Daryl Howard All Rights Reserved.
For more information go to: DarylHoward.com

Stone, Donna M.
1. Inspirational 2. Christian Life 3. Memoir

Dedication

This book is for you, Mom. Without you at the helm, my life would never have blossomed as it did. Your never-ending encouragement, strength and conviction molded my perseverance to follow my dreams. Godly wisdom was instilled with every heartbeat as my footprints in the sands of life tell a story that I thank you for, every day.

About the Cover

The cover artwork is an original creation from artist Daryl Howard created for the author for this book. All rights reserved.

The Flame of Grace

Original Collage

Featuring 22k gold leaf; cut rubies from Jaipur, India; Earth pigments from Mt. St. Helens; WBP segments from "Fragile Brilliance" by Daryl Howard, circa 1991; antique kimono fabric, circa 1940; shibori, circa 1900; antique silkscreen paper, circa 1940

Table of Contents

Foreword

The apostle Paul wrote to the church that he founded in Ephesus admonishing them to, *"grow up in every way into him who is the head, into Christ"* (Ephesians 4.15). In order for them to be *grown up* or *mature* in their discipleship to Jesus, they needed to both receive and exercise the various spiritual gifts of leadership that Jesus himself would give to various persons in their community of faith. All of these gifts—apostles, prophets, evangelists, pastors and teachers (vs. 10) have a common purpose: *"to equip the saints for the work of ministry, for building up the body of Christ, until all of us come to the unity of the faith and of the knowledge of the Son of God, to maturity, to the measure of the full stature of Christ"* (vs. 12-13).

Notice the progression. Leaders are to "equip" the members of the church so that each person will be built up to fully embody all that Jesus desires to accomplish in their lives. This "building up" will bring them in this life time to "maturity" and it will at the same time place them in the great living body of the whole wonderful reality of God's church. The goal Paul communicates here is that all of the ministry that Jesus desires for his people will be unfolding in that local group of believers in Ephesus. They have a mission to fulfill which is to make known the mystery of the good news of Jesus (6.19) to the world about them. The mission requires them to live as mature women and men of God.

Paul's original language for what is translated in English as "to equip" has some expansive connotations. First of all it is something that is accomplished rather than an endless, ongoing process. This of course, should give us hope in that maturity can indeed be gifted to us during this lifetime. But where it gets really interesting is in what the word actually meant. The leaders of the church are to make sure that everything needful is put in place in believer's lives. Every believer is to be "mended" to Christ in such a way as to have the Lord's standard of maturity thriving in their lives.

This "mending" is precisely where Donna Stone's personal testimony and teaching come into play. If we are to be mended, that is properly put back together, repaired, joined to our Head, and knit in love to one another, then some profound actions of God's grace are going to have to pour into our broken, unhinged lives and repair that which has been corrupted by original sin. Proper relationship with our God will have to be restored through the gracious sacrifice of Jesus and loving relationship with one another will have to be established through the unifying love of the Holy Spirit.

We need guides for this mending work of God. We need mature teachers who themselves have been mended by Jesus and then sent out to provide the thread and needle to mend fellow members of the body of Jesus into the fullness of his love. *The Flame of Grace* is a sewing kit as such. It is a text written from the very pages of the rich life and experience of one of God's beloved shepherds.

All worthy guides accomplish a goal. They not only speak to us about the way forward, but they also come along side of us and help us move into the goal of maturity. Donna Stone is such a guide and she walks right beside us by opening her own life and then by applying the teaching of our Lord and Savior Jesus to all of our lives. There is healing, instruction, and inspiration in this sweet account from a Christian nurse, veteran, wife, mother, grandmother, teacher and pastor.

This text starts where most of us need to start as we move toward hope and healing: with the anchoring reality that we are created in the image and likeness of God and are pursued by the love of God. Our deepest reality--the very gift of who we are--is rooted in the Trinity. Childhood deformation and wounds throughout life are inevitable, but as Stone writes:

To be a creature of God holds an expectation, an unrealized fulfillment that can only be satisfied by God. God is every bit good and desires our central focus to be heavenward as we learn our heavenly potential. I believe that God's view of me is my human potential fully realized. What would that look like? I envisioned a balance of body, mind, and spirit as peace began to be revealed in my behavior and body language.

The human person fully alive in God is a historic Christian understanding that Donna Stone unfolds for the reader throughout her text. Her honesty in sharing the fires of her own life, her grounding in solid discipleship practice, her excellent inclusion of helpful insights from the human life sciences, and her outstanding questions and resources at the end of each chapter offer individuals and groups a pathway for healing of body, mind, and spirit.

By sharing her life testimony, including the wounds, failure, fears, the difficult family dynamics, Donna Stone has given true testimony to how the loving presence of God has met her at each step along the way. As one who personally knows the rest of the story in her grace-filled life, I can also share that the grace and healing that came through the fires of her life have all resulted in her stepping into the mission of God for the world. From wounding through healing to discipleship and service she reflects for us the path of life in Jesus our Lord. This text will be a blessing for many upon that path.

Stephen L. Martyn
Associate Professor of Spiritual Formation
Asbury Theological Seminary

INTRODUCTION

You have chosen this story of my journey as a starting place, possibly to find an answer to unanswered questions about yourself. Whether you are a nurse or have similar gifted-ness, I believe my story will have insights for you. Looking back on my 70-plus years, I will unfold for you some of the layers of the onion that were peeled away through many tears, to bring me to the God-given joy that I live today. In a study of my own life, I will take you now through my "drivenness"-my outward behaviors that covered an internal need -- to a wholeness that can only be realized once the balance of Body - Mind - Spirit has been reached. This wholeness is based upon our creation as a Child of God and our intended purpose, which holds all that is needed for a solid foundation of living a life of personal fulfillment. My firm belief is that our lifetime is spent in search of the person that God created us to be -- a mirror image of the love that is beyond comprehension and certainly timeless as God is timeless.

Reflecting on Jesus' short journey here on earth, I will replay for you the pain, suffering, hope and ultimate joy that awaited me. In my early formative years, I had insights that led me from one discovery to another, all of which affected my self-perception and trials that came later.

As a young adult I became aware that choices are everywhere as we grow and mature. I chose to become a health care worker, a nurse, to use my gifts and graces in caring for those entrusted to me. Spanning all echelons of care, from the smallest air-transportable hospital in the field to the largest 1000-bed facility, military nursing was my forté. A natural affinity for innovation led me to areas of discovery where new ideas could be designed and implemented.

In teaching skilled nurses, I recognized that personality played the greatest role in a person's self-perception and consequently his or her care-giving. Understanding our "self" is the greatest key to understanding others. As consultant for the highly developed Meyers-Briggs Temperament Sorter and later, the Birkman Assessment Tool, I became particularly cued in to stress behaviors and how they invoked predictable responses within a person's environment and among co-workers. I then expanded the study of stress behaviors to a group of twenty nurses with very interesting results.

My graduate work was spent in the study of guidance and counseling, followed by a wealth of courses in organizational behavior of healthcare workers. A firm believer in leadership potential, I concentrated on educating the leaders.

Throughout my life, my love for God has and always will be my driving force. Yet, without the help of my mentors, my counselors, friends and family, I would not have been able to pick up and look at the pieces that God pushed me to examine. From wounded-ness to winning, I believe God's guidance has informed and protected me. From heartache to reward, the Almighty has set me free.

My story, I believe, is more typical than atypical, more widely experienced than unique, and more promising than we can imagine. I pray that you take time to appreciate your God-given beauty and potential, as a gift to those in your sphere of influence. I pray for your openness to fresh ideas. May you be led to a new way of giving, and forgiving as God intends.

CHAPTER ONE
GOD'S CREATION

I was the seventh in a line of thirty-two women climbing the steps to the campus chapel. It was June 1970 and the commissioning ceremony for graduating baccalaureate nurses was about to take place. As I neared the double doors, I could see Mom and Dad peering around the crowds. We processed in to the front pews and carefully, prayerfully sang the selected hymns. The message given by the Dean of the School of Nursing readied us for the years ahead, for our responsibility as patient advocate, scientist, pastor, and confidante. I never viewed the position as having so much authority, but I began to see the meaning of a caring nurse from the patient's point of view. As we filed into two columns along the center aisle facing each other, candles were distributed to each of us. The chapel lights were dimmed and the Chaplain read the nurses creed. I looked at the light and it was Florence Nightingale's lamp. I recalled her pioneer spirit and knew I was in the right job. The scripture passage *"Thy Word is a lamp unto my feet and a light unto my path" Psalm (119:10)* filled my thoughts. I would experience two graduations-the formal university or "head" graduation and this one, the "heart" graduation.

* * *

Leaving the nurture of my home and entering the world of nursing, though I was petrified, I was driven to prove myself. With schooling finally at an end, all the hopes and dreams for my future were taking form. There was a peace and contentment about completing such a challenging chapter of my life. As I looked back over all the college courses and the endless hours of study, the candlelight ceremony where my commitment to nursing was affirmed, put it all in perspective for me. Finally...I was ready to take care of patients! In the hospital, although I first noticed cultural differences -- in patients, in supervisors, in language and in thought, I soon learned that there was a same-ness. Despite the differences, all people had a great deal in common emotionally. Created with a mind to question, I knew that there might come a time when following my will, my thoughts or my decisions might alter their view of wholeness. My first challenge—to see how my world view of 'wholeness' would intersect with theirs. How would my understanding of body/mind/spirit balance agree or conflict with theirs? In my understanding, Biblical wholeness is the entirety of an individual that is in agreement with God the Father. It comprises the physical body, soul and spirit that is born anew, operating as one system in intimacy, trust, dependence and obedience to God.[1] As we operate in wholeness, I believe that we are functioning as we were originally created to function. God's plan for Biblical wholeness includes our taking personal responsibility for our physical body so that we may fully serve the Lord. We are the temple of the Living God *(1Cor 6:19-20)*.

I wondered how I could make a difference in the short duration of a person's hospital stay. It seemed to me like a perfect opportunity to teach, to be a patient's advocate linking the care of the caregiver to the needs of the patient. Compassion, mercy and grace deeply affected the care that I gave on a daily basis. God does not change. Humanity is given repeated opportunities to step out of its comfort zone to serve others. It takes courage. It is our individual journey that we have experienced through God to take us to a new level of caring. For until we internalize the true meaning of mercy and compassion and therefore allow it into our very being, we are only partially allowing God's healing touch to work through us. I believe that God's love is unwavering. As often as we struggle to find our own way and are swayed from the path of love, God covers us with his cloak of comfort *"...as free, yet not using liberty as a cloak for vice, but as bondservants of God" (Exodus 16:8)* and pledges the covenant of eternal love for us. Such is parental love. If there were no choices, the free will that God has promised could not be exercised.

A great philosopher and spiritual master Meister Eckhart, teaches that there are four reasons that "giving birth" to compassion is the finest birthing we can do. He states "God the Creator, alone, is the compassionate one" and compassion was present at creation so we are drawn to it. There are four reasons that call us to compassion, he says. Compassion: 1) ... triumphs over enemies, 2) ...renders us divine and clothed in our proper divinity, 3) ... directs a person to relationship with his or her fellow human beings by way of justice, and 4) ... bestows heavenly blessings on us all therefore beginning the end time which is the time of our final salvation, healing and beatitude or full happiness.[3]

Early in my career I questioned everything, not yet seeing the complexity of or the connection between the body, mind and spirit. I had a seedling of understanding of biblical wholeness, but have come to understand it more fully today. "Biblical wholeness" refers to the extent to which the individual is in agreement with God the Creator. It comprises the physical body, the soul and the spirit that is born anew, operating as one harmonious system in intimacy, trust, dependence, and obedience to God the Father in cooperation with the power of the Holy Spirit. My natural inclination was to seek answers from God's Word, so I looked to the Bible where I began my search in the creation story of the Biblical Scriptures. There I found scriptures that spoke to me from the Book of Genesis that answered questions about the origin of humankind, other life forms, and sin and evil. God's mercy, compassion and reassurance are again reaffirmed in the First Book of Corinthians, sometimes called the book of love...

"Or do you not know that your body is the temple of the Holy Spirit who is in you, whom you have from God, and you are not your own? For you were bought at a price; therefore, glorify God in your body and in your spirit, which are God's." (1 Corinthians 6:19-20)

I find divine inspiration in the Genesis account. With God the center of all that we enjoy, the Alpha, I believe only The Creator's majestic intellect could devise a creation with such purpose. According to this creation account, humankind is the highlight of the six days of creation.

"Let Us make man in Our image, according to Our likeness; let them have dominion over the fish of the sea, over the birds of the air, and over the cattle, over all the earth and over every creeping thing that creeps on the earth." (Genesis 1:26.)

The message of John 4:25 taught me that God is Spirit and those who worship Him must worship Him in spirit and in truth. Though made in God's image *(Genesis 1:26)* we are not equal to the Almighty. What struck me as a young woman was the absolute reassurance that God was in control. Isaiah 45:18 states, *"He made the world to be lived in, not to be an empty chaos,"* reassuring me that God is a God of order. Being made in God's image gives each human being individual worth and value, which means you and I are priceless to God.

As I walked the hospital halls one night, I remember being alarmed at my worry concerning one particular patient's condition, stressing over what I would do about his pain, I found myself extra-vigilant, tense for some reason but did not understand why. I peered out of the window at the end of the hall and as the sun rose in the distance, I knew that ultimately I could depend on God to guide and care for me as well as for that patient. If God could create the universe, I felt sure that The Almighty could get me through this one night shift.

In the years that followed, I grew to appreciate my life more and more, feeling in-tune with patients who had experienced suffering. I was able to help them. Naturally tolerant of negativity in others, I could see beyond their behavior, trusting that they didn't really mean to act or react so negatively. The opportunity came during that first year when I took the plunge and joined the Air Force Nurse Corps. At the age of twenty-three, my boundless energy was still not contained and I thought that travel to new and different lands would bring excitement and more challenges. Since that very first trip, I have enjoyed both planned as well as spontaneous travel to exciting cultures and foreign lands.

It wasn't until I observed God's creation in the field of obstetrics that I began to realize the plan that God might be revealing to me. There is nothing quite so delicate or fragile as a new life. To see a newborn infant from the delivery to the mother's arms is an awesome experience. Labor and Delivery allows much time for waiting...waiting with questions, waiting with hopes and waiting with a plan for the greatest mystery of life to be revealed. God chose for Jesus to arrive in this world as an infant. His birth now had new meaning for me.

In this day of self-sufficiency, a newborn portrays the opposite-absolute, total dependence. Though there are instinctive behaviors-the rooting reflex to find food and the startle reflex signaling danger, the absolute need that a child has for his/her mother spells loudly and clearly the tender nature of God's newest creation. Gradually I was learning that I was more dependent upon God than I realized. The power of the love surrounding us daily was and continues to be overwhelming to me.

This study will explain how I became aware of God's presence in my life, even before I realized it. Since I was awakening to spiritual hunger, my pastor recommended that I read the works of Meister Eckhart, a fourteenth century Dominican priest and beloved mystic. He is a creation-centered theologian, a guide for those individuals open to a biblically-grounded spiritual journey.

"The creative Word of God describes the blessing that creation is. It flows out but remains within."[4] Creativity is the work of God in us. God is the Creator and we, in God's image, follow in those footsteps. In Meister Eckhart's eyes, creative artistic work is the only work that satisfies, for it is the only work that brings to the surface our individual giftedness. It flows out, but remains within. It is the 'flowing out' that all creative people must discipline themselves to do in order that beauty and blessing be shared.[5]

All of creation is a Divine Blessing. God permeates all things and renders all things equal at the level of being. "A new definition of humanity is suggested: a human being is a blessing destined to bless other beings in a conscious way by way of creativity and compassion. Other creatures on this earth bless the rest of us unconsciously."[6] For Meister Eckhart, God is not "out there"; God is in us and we are in God. This theology emphasizes the omnipresence of God.[7]

Eternal life is understood by Eckhart to be in the "now". If heaven has not already begun for us, then our personal view is the major obstacle.

God's love for me was and is so empowering, so all-encompassing that I saw "nursing" as the natural framework God chose for me to understand my self, my world and my mission in life. Discovering the nature of God was building my trust that the Creator was in control of every area of my life. The universe bears witness to the enormity of God's presence and I found myself fascinated with the complexities of creation. As I grew in the knowledge of the Almighty and the meaning of creation, I marveled at the avenues that God chose to help me and to offer new sources of healing. In my celebrations, I felt that God cheered me on; as I stumbled and fell, I knew it must have been God helping me to my feet to try again. As the storms of life wreaked their havoc, God granted me peace. At times, the storm within me was calmed and at times the storms that surrounded me were calmed. God has been my constant through all of it.

I am absolutely convinced that until we know our limitations, there is little hope of really knowing God. The day that I realized that I could not accomplish everything myself, but more importantly, did not have to do it all myself, was the day I began to realize how stretched I had allowed myself to become. I was exhausted, and probably exhausting others. I believe God's promises for each of us today--*"even before you were born"* (Isaiah 44:2). There was a plan for all mankind and there is a plan for us today. Because God knew us even before we were born, the plan for the spreading of the kingdom requires knowledge of the Word. Throughout the generations, it has been, and is up to us to receive and share the nature of a loving God. It is in looking to God for guidance for a better view of our life's goal, that we learn Who, and Whose we are. Given that we are a reflection of God *"made in His image" (Genesis 1:26, 27)* it is incumbent upon us as followers to turn and seek a changed heart. A changed heart can only come through complete surrender, surrender to God's will and surrender to the process of "becoming."

As we learn about ourselves and become aware of strengths and weaknesses, a separation is noticed between the inward (spiritual) and outward (physical) components of our being. We are human beings and capable of rational, self directed thoughts. In other words, we have to "think" about an action before we "perform" the action. The spiritual dimension is within, not visible to the outside world. The only way to get in touch with our spiritual dimension is to develop spiritual insight. When we come to a greater understanding of God and the universe, we are petitioned to come as children. There is a reason for this. Children are open-minded--open to learning, open to changes in their thinking and therefore more open to God.

It is with new eyes, eyes of faith that God creates in us a new heart. How can I be used effectively until I understand my own weaknesses? Try as I may, there will be people placed in my path who bring out the absolute worst in me. The sooner I learn the lesson of turning over my will to God's greater will, the sooner I am able to move on. For it is in my weakness that God is strong. At my weakest point, God used me. Time and time again I branched out on my own, without ever asking God to help me see the plan. The Creator was using His people as instruments to narrow the path, my mom in the case of my failed business venture, my fellow retiree friends when I wouldn't just settle down and relax. I was so independent; I had to do it all myself.

Becoming a new creation opened me to the possibility of seeing my blind spots. God sent the helpers. My Creator knew my needs much better than I did myself, and met them knowing full well that I would grow as I was nurtured. I had to first admit that I didn't know it all and basically needed God's leadership. Through divine intervention, the messages were loud and clear about those who "hurt" me, in both my perception and in my physical being. God gave me a new understanding of everything I questioned each time that I was able to submit to divine guidance and admit my errors.

A friend suggested that I take a weekend away, a spiritual retreat weekend. As I proceeded with the application, an interesting calendar of events unfolded. While having a manicure one afternoon, I noticed a book resting on the hairdresser's stand. It had to do with salvation. As I read the words, a thought struck me like a firecracker-was I saved? How would I know it? Who would know if I was? Tears welled up in my eyes, the lady returned and when she asked if I was all right, I couldn't speak so I pointed to the book. She asked if I would like to pray. I responded yes and she invited me to accompany her to the back of the shop. She prayed for my understanding, for healing direction to be given, and for a peace in the days ahead. When I explained the three-day retreat to her, she asked how I would prepare for it. I admitted that I didn't know. She recommended a cassette tape describing solitude with God. This became a tremendous focusing agent and she asked me when I would have some "alone time" to prepare. The following Tuesday at 9:30 AM, I was headed for the lake, a time away and a time for my total focus to be on God. I took only my Bible.

Opening first to the Table of Contents, I asked God to show me what to read. Individual books were highlighted and as I read each one, I was taught the precepts I needed most. Loudly and clearly, I received the message, *"Be still and know that I am God." (Psalm 46:10a)* This spoke to me; I was frazzled. Tears were streaming down my face. I opened my eyes and realized that I was kneeling beside the rock where I originally sat. My legs felt bound and I couldn't move. I cried out for God to help. As I opened my eyes and looked to the left, there stood a huge goose a mere eighteen inches away. He looked at me with the calmest eyes. I didn't want to scare him away, so I continued to pray and thanked God for sending a sign to comfort me. A second goose joined him briefly, and then flew away. I have never forgotten the powerful message of that day. God is in control; I am not. Little did I realize the giant step I had taken in my faith-walk. If this was any indication of the "walk" to come, I'd better fasten my seatbelt for the ride of my life.

After a twenty-three year Air Force career, I was a mom in retirement with no new goal and a recent business failure that left me devastated. My marriage was rocky at best and my husband couldn't help because his flying schedule took him overseas three weeks a month.

Wait a minute! I graduated from nursing school I am earning my own money, working for a living…and nothing had changed. The tension level that existed before was still there. Now I am faced with another decision. Is it the environment? The answer for me was "yes." Work had not changed; my surroundings at work had not changed, but the same triggers to my emotional self were still as strong. I remember vividly feeling the pressure of a decision that I had made in conversation with a laboring patient. I advised her to come to the hospital to have her contractions evaluated rather than stay at home. This decision resulted in a supervisory reprimand and me going home in tears again. What had I done wrong? The long and short of it was "nothing." I was reacting to being corrected. Rather than meeting me with a 'teaching moment' response, my supervisor laughed and said I jumped the gun by requiring the patient to come in early. This was a symptom of a deeper issue for me. My fear of making a mistake made me hesitant to reach out. There is little wonder that I decided to join the Air force—tension at home, tension at work!

SUMMARY
CHAPTER ONE - GOD'S CREATION

The universe was shaped for a purpose: to be the home of humankind. However vast the world may be, God cares most about living beings. Psalm 104 reviews God's creative acts and praises The Almighty for forming our world as a habitation for living things both great and small. The earth and all its creatures were given unto man's keeping. To us then came both the gift and the responsibility.

Meister Eckhart became a friar and dedicated his life to the study of God's creation and the spirituality that molds human beings. His is a creation theology. A study of his teachings, sermons and stories reveals a solid knowledge of Biblical truths, wisdom and a perception of life that applied 14th century understandings to present day growth. In his perception, God can be experienced: 1) in Creation, 2) by "letting go and letting be," 3) in breakthrough and birth to self, and 4) as compassion and social justice. In his purview, a person progresses through these four stages during his lifetime, culminating in a final understanding of God's intent, our purpose here on earth, and God's ultimate justice in meeting the needs of society as we know it.

As faith guides our learning, the spiritual party of our body - mind - spirit balance opens new doors to acting and interacting with God and then with our neighbors. Balance in our daily lives is God's goal -- total surrender and obedience to the law of love that was laid down centuries ago. Relationship issues are the most taxing and also the most rewarding of our human existence. Until we admit that only God holds the keys to our total understanding and guidance, we risk a life of quiet abandon, relinquishing all hope of entering the Promised Land.

QUESTIONS
CHAPTER ONE - GOD'S CREATION

1. Is it possible to reach Biblical Wholeness by obtaining body-mind-spirit balance? How is God's grace the enabler?

2. In his creation theology, the philosopher-teacher Meister Eckhart lists four reasons that draw us toward compassion. Briefly describe each of the four areas.

3. Do we have spiritual responsibilities? To whom are we accountable? How are we accountable?

4. Discuss surrender and obedience to God's law of love.

RESOURCES

1. Marill, Marcia, Experiencing Biblical Wholeness, Columbus, Georgia: Brentwood Christian Press, 2001. Page 13

2 Ibid, Page 12

3 Fox, Matthew, Breakthrough, Meister Eckhart's Creation Spirituality in New Translation. New York: Doubleday Image Books, 1980. Page 9

4. Ibid, Page 9

5. Ibid, Page 44

6. Ibid, Page 44

CHAPTER TWO
CHILD OF GOD

Meeting my eighty-eight-year-old friend, Katie, was no accident. Bible study classmates for two years, I learned that she spent her early career as a nurse. She quickly became my mentor and confidante as we shared spiritual journeys and exchanged insights into the special meaning of the term "Child of God." Katie and her husband reared four boys, blessed in the years that followed with twelve grandchildren. The "Katie Connection" was pivotal for me as I grappled with God's Word and sought to understand the chapters of my life. She was 30+ years my senior, and I would soon learn, the teacher that God placed in my path for that time. The following is her response to my question "What spiritual values do you desire to pass on to your grandchildren?"

Through Grandma's Eyes
(Katie's response)

The backgrounds and experiences that mold grandparents are as varied as their personalities. Their responses to change in culture, environment, education, philosophy, and life situations reflect their basic ideologies. Each has developed his or her own understanding of good and evil as well as their concept of God. In Deuteronomy 11:18-21,

"you shall therefore lay up these words of mine in your heart and in your soul and you shall bind them as a sign on your hand and they shall be as front lets between your eyes. You shall teach them to your children, talking of them when you are sitting in your house and when you are walking by the way, and when you lie down and when you rise. You shall write them on the doorposts of your house and on your gates, that your days and the days of your children may be multiplied in the end that the LORD swore to your fathers to give them, as long as the heavens are above the earth."

It was You, God, who formed me in my mother's womb.

"For you formed my inward parts; you knitted me together in my mother's womb. I praise you, for I am fearfully and wonderfully made. Wonderful are your works, my soul knows it very well. My frame was not hidden from you, when I was being made in secret, intricately woven in the depths of the earth. Your eyes saw my unformed substance, in your book were written, every one of them, the days that were formed for me, when as yet there were not of them." (Psalm 139:13-16)

As a Christian, "born again" grandmother, I have come to know that "By the power of the Holy Spirit I strive to know and pursue the heart and will of the Triune God. I have been a grandchild, child and parent myself as well as a grandmother to twelve grandchildren and one great grandchild."

"What spiritual values do I desire to pass on to my grandchildren?" True spirituality is what the Holy Spirit teaches us as we read the Bible and pray. Through this divine truth and revelation given by the Holy Spirit, our daily lives are guided. So much of spirituality is experienced and not taught. It is not my responsibility to "save" my grandchildren since that is the Lord's business. It is my duty to live a Godly life, share my salvation story, pray for my grandchildren and look for those teachable moments making sure that I am passing on what God desires. I can act as a filter and through my choice of books, music and movies that I give them that my values will be reflected.

Fascination with God's creation never ceases to amaze the interested. Each egg that a woman carries is present at her own birth.[1] This miracle of reproduction points further to our God who has had a plan for each of us from the beginning of time. The sanctity of each life should be preserved and cherished. This value of human life must be communicated to our granddaughters and grandsons at an early age. It gives them a basis for self-worth and a foundation for making moral decisions.

We have the capacity to communicate with God due to the sacred relationship that is offered by our Creator. Being born sinful, we must make the choice to follow our Lord and Savior in total surrender and accept the work of the Holy Spirit in our lives. Our grandchildren watch every move we make. As I nurture them in Christian values, they will hopefully begin to understand the magnitude of God's love.

There is no potential for imparting spiritual values if there is no relationship with my grandchildren. Trust and harmony are crucial to developing the underpinnings of this relationship and it is best established by the investment of "time." The activities need not be expensive or complicated. They can be as simple as taking short shopping trips, spending the afternoon cooking and baking, or having short overnighters at Grandma's house.

This is when the valuable role of "listener" is so crucial and we become the bridge between generations. This is not the time to sermonize, but rather to model both behaviors and beliefs that are important to the next generation. It is now that we serve as role models whether we are conscious of it or not. Impressionable minds will be watching to see if we read our Bibles, quote scripture or attend church. They will notice if we pray or say the blessing. They will see the choices that we make, the way we conduct ourselves; the way we spend our time, the friends we choose, and the books we read.

We first pass on a great deal of spiritual sensitivity to our own children. Making ourselves "available" as they begin to rear their own families gives us the opportunity to help in ways only a grandparent can. I remember the struggle that I had when I nursed my first son-the first time is never easy. Almost three decades later, my daughter-in-law was able to encourage this same granddaughter as she began nursing my first great-grandchild. We should not take lightly how we can pass on encouragement and hope to future generations by simply sharing what experience has taught us.

Our grandchildren may not seem fully receptive to all that we share spiritually and we may not even see the results of our efforts during our lifetime. Even though every grandmother is not in the same place in her walk with the Lord, she still has a great deal of wisdom and knowledge to share with our youth. There is wisdom with age and future generations will harvest the fruit from the seeds we have planted. We must realize that we are helping to prepare a solid foundation upon which they can build their lives. It is my privilege to pass on what I have lived and tested.

(Signed)
Katie May

It was you, God, who *"fashioned me in my mother's womb."* *(Psalm 139:13)* I will attempt to order my thoughts, as I believe God intended. As Katie's wisdom sank into my soul, I learned that each and every generation is one of hope, health and choice. Born as dependent, the degrees of security we experience in all relationships throughout our lifetime are impacted by our total dependence at birth. We are solely dependent upon our mother for safety, security and survival. Regardless of race, culture or location in the world, God's well-intentioned actions have eternal significance, generation to generation. Assessment of learning during the course of our lifetime, focuses on the general categories of infancy, preschool and kindergarten to 12th grade, early adult (ages 18-30 years), middle age (30-50 years) and later life (50+ years). Designed by God, we are created by Perfection itself. Filled with goodness as God is only good and building on our unique familial characteristics, we begin life in search of "completeness". Biblical wholeness is sought throughout our lifetime, rejuvenated as we become aware of God's plan and purpose. Early childhood growth and development theories of Drs. Henri Brazelton, Jean Piaget, Abraham Maslow and Carl Jung provide a sequential timeline of human learning. In conclusion, I compare Katie's insight to Meister Eckhart's view of the body and soul. Spiritual values and responsibilities learned in the family are described as they affect the special heritage of God's people.

As children of God, humans are unique. Promised in the Holy Bible, we are created to love God, given the choice to respond to that implanted love, to build relationship with our Creator. Infants are born "ready" - ready to learn, ready to explore and ready to begin the early sequence of "taking in" what we developmentally are capable of learning. The Brazelton Neonatal Assessment Index describes an infant's competencies and individuality, measuring eighteen behaviors and reflex items designed to examine the newborn's physiological, motor state and social capacities. Maslow's hierarchy of needs, Piaget's cognitive development and Carl Jung's theory of personality and spirituality all deal with motivational needs and their sequencing.

From the literature, I reviewed the top four researchers in the field of developmental psychology-Drs. Henri Brazelton, Jean Piaget, Abraham Maslow and Carl Jung. Dr. Bravelton's work examines the first few months of the baby's life and is significant because of its multi-cultural adaptation. His Newborn Behavioral Observation (NBO) tool examines the infant's physiological, motor state, and social capacities during the first two months of life. The goal of the system is to promote the development of supportive relationships between the infant, family and the clinician. By the third month of life, the examiner has a behavioral "portrait" of the infant, describing the baby's strengths, adaptive responses and possible vulnerabilities. Caregiving strategies are aimed at enhancing the earliest relationship between babies and parents. (Harvard Medical School.)[2]

Jean Piaget believed that children adapt their thinking to include new ideas through four stages of development. Assimilation (incorporating new information to existing knowledge) and accommodation (adjustment to new knowledge) operate even in the very young infant's life.[2]

Dr. Piaget describes four developmental stages:

1. *Sensori-motor* (birth to two years) when an infant constructs an understanding of the world by coordinating sensory experiences such as seeing and hearing, with physical actions.

2. *Pre-operational* (two to seven years) when children begin to represent the world with words, images and drawings.

3. *Concrete operational stage* (seven to eleven years) when children can perform operations and logical reasoning replaces intuitive thought.

4. *Formal operational stage* (eleven to fifteen years) when the individual moves beyond concrete experiences and thinks in abstract, more logical terms. He or she starts to deal with abstractions and how things might be, but are not.[3]

Dr. Jean Piaget further reveals how infants strive to control their motor system. Once this task is managed, the focus settles on his or her "state". State is a key developmental concept that describes levels of consciousness, ranging from quiet sleep to full cry. The infant's ability to control his or her state enables the child to process and respond to information from the caregiving environment. When the infant's autonomic, motor and state systems are in equilibrium, he or she is ready to interact socially, the ultimate developmental task.

Professor Abraham Maslow, a humanistic psychologist, developed a theory of personality that is understandable, practical and accurately resonates with the experiences of most people. Humanists focus on potentials.[4] Professor Maslow developed a hierarchy of needs beginning with instinctive, the equivalent of instincts in animals. Beyond the basic level, he believed that higher levels do exist. These higher levels include understanding, aesthetic appreciation and purely spiritual needs. Within the basic five needs, the person does not feel the second need until the demands of the first have been satisfied, nor the third until the second has been satisfied and so on.

The basic needs are:

1. *Physiologic* - Biological - for oxygen, food, water, and a relatively constant body temperature. These are the strongest needs since survival depends upon them.

2. *Safety* - When the physiologic level has been satisfied and no longer controls thoughts and behaviors, the need for security can become active. Adults have little awareness of their security needs except in times of emergency or periods of disorganization in the social structure.

Children often display signs of insecurity and a need to be safe.

3. *Love, Affection and Belongingness* - As the safety and physiological needs are met, those for love, affection and belongingness can emerge. Dr. Maslow states that people seek to overcome feelings of loneliness and alienation. Both "giving" and "receiving" love; affection and belongingness comprise this level of need. When these are frustrated, the person feels inferior, weak, helpless and worthless.

4. *Esteem* - When the first three levels of need are satisfied, esteem can become dominant. Humans have a need for a stable, firmly based, high level of self-respect and respect from others.

5. *Self-Actualization* - At the culmination of schooling or special training, a person enters his or her chosen field - the one he or she feels "born to do." This implies an openness that contrasts with the introspection that can be a pre-requisite for great artistic self-expression.[4]

6. *Homeostasis* - The balance reached when all levels of need have been satisfied.

Often represented by a pyramid, the lower levels represent the lower needs, ascending toward the upper point of self-actualization. Dr. Maslow believed that the only hindrance to people moving in the direction of self-actualization is from the barriers placed by society. He saw all needs as essentially survival needs. Even love and esteem are needed for maintenance of health. Under stressful conditions, or when survival is threatened, it is quite possible to "regress" to a lower need level.

To a point, Dr. Maslow's theory appears complete, however, the hierarchy of needs is incomplete from a biblical standpoint since it denies the most fundamental need of all, an individual relationship with the Divine Savior, Jesus Christ. Donald Kraybill, in his book, *The Upside Down Kingdom*, examines the way that God's kingdom inverts the values that drive our society. Kingdom values challenge the patterns of social life taken for granted in modern culture.[6]

Dr. Jung has opened our eyes to the differences between child development and adult development. Children clearly emphasize differentiation in their learning, i.e. separating one thing from another. They actively seek diversity. Adults, on the other hand, search for the connections between things; seek to learn how things fit together, interact and contribute to the whole. They want to make sense of it, to find the meaning of it, the purpose of it all. Children unravel the world; adults try to knit it back together.[7] Dr. Jung's theory stands out from all others in his description of the collective unconscious, also known as "psychic inheritance."[8] The contents of the collective unconscious are called archetypes They are referred to as dominants, images, and mythological or primordial images. An archetype is an unlearned tendency to experience things in a certain way. This archetype has no form of its own, but acts as an "organizing principle" on things we see or do.

The most important archetype of all is the self. The self is the ultimate unity of the personality and is symbolized by the circle, the cross, and the mandala, figures that Dr. Jung used in meditation. These drew a person's attention to the center. Known for its unique descriptions, the Meyers-Briggs Personality Type Indicator is used extensively for assessment and testing. Four scales measure the amount of Extroversion/Introversion,

Sensing/Intuiting, Thinking/Feeling, Judging/Perception that a person reveals. The sixteen "types" then become an invitation for individuals to search themselves, determine their superior function, the supporting or secondary function and the tertiary or inferior function.[10]

"Biblical Wholeness" refers to the state of the individual that is in agreement with the Father. It comprises the physical body, soul and the spirit that is born anew, through cooperation with the power of the Holy Spirit.[11]

"Or do you not know that your body is the temple of the Holy Spirit who is in you, whom you have from God, and you are not your own? For you were bought at a price; therefore, glorify God in your body and in your spirit, which are God's." (1 Corinthians 6:19-20)

The family, biblically speaking, holds ultimate responsibility for the teaching of its youth. Depending upon the "state" of the mother (body-mind-spirit), a certain environment is automatically set up that surrounds the developing fetus. Babies hold in them the DNA of their parents, along with the family's generational uniqueness. As we grow within the home, teachings reveal a product comprised of prior experiences and the family dynamics that follow. The Book of Genesis is foundational, clearly describing our beginning. God so completely loved us that all of our surroundings were created with beauty. Adam and Eve were surrounded with beauty in the Garden of Eden. When they succumbed to the temptation to defy God, that choice ultimately changed the course of humanity. How sad that such total beauty was marred by disobedience, conceit, hurt and anger.

Our physical body is a marvelous work of art. The body systems, just one act of God's perfect design, reveal twelve perfectly connected, interdependent systems to sustain life. The twelve body systems include: 1) Respiratory, 2) Circulatory, 3) Reproductive, 4) Gastrointestinal, 5) Renal, 6) Immune, 7) Muscular, 8) Skeletal, 9) Endocrine, 10) Nervous, 11) Sensory, and 12) Integumentary (skin). "The human body works in a precise and orderly fashion to display the perfect divine design. We are responsible to be good stewards of the gift of our body. A teachable, open heart is critical to our understanding of God's laws. If we neglect the laws of God, the natural man will again suffer the consequences."[12]

> "but let a man examine himself, and so let him eat of the bread and drink of the cup. For he who eats and drinks in an unworthy manner, eats and drinks judgment to himself, not discerning the Lord's body." (1 Corinthians 11:28-29)

The Bible spells out God's intention for maintaining our health. Scriptures from the Books of Leviticus and Deuteronomy define health ordinances and laws for the consumption and preparation of foods. Choosing healthy foods begins with having scriptural knowledge of the types of food that are good for us.[14] In Biblical times, the principal nourishment of all cultural classes were produced from wheat oats, barley and rye, with rice available along the coast. Lentils, beans, chickpeas, onions and leeks provided vegetables rich in the vitamins necessary for healing and growth. The well-to-do class ate meat regularly. In their diet, fowl, fish, ham and mutton were available.[15] Grapes provided wines and bees produced excellent honey. The average person's diet consisted of grains, vegetables, olive oil and dairy products.[16]

As a living temple, our bodies are truly dependent upon us to choose healthy foods and to exercise. As Jesus reminded us, it was not the food that made us spiritually unclean, though it can make us physically or emotionally sick. Likewise, self-destructive choices harm us emotionally, for our bodies were meant to be in motion. Worldliness and sin make us spiritually unclean.[17] Jewish dietary laws were set for specific health issues--matters of cleanliness, food preparation techniques and healthy habits. The fat of animal meat, for instance, houses ingested toxins of that animal. Logically, this would be a poor choice for consumption. Additionally, animal fat directly raises serum cholesterol by clogging the arteries. There are healthier, more nutrient-rich and tastier foods available for us today, just as in biblical times. Wholeness depends on the body - mind - spirit balance.

"*Thy kingdom is not of this world,*" *(John 18:36)* explains that life under God's control is strikingly different from a life seeking to fulfill and satisfy its own needs. In fact, Jesus Christ makes it even more clear by advising his disciples to not be concerned with food, clothing, housing, comfort and money when doing his Father's work.

> "*And he said to them, 'Take nothing for the journey, neither staffs nor bag, nor bread, nor money; and do not have two tunics apiece. Whatever house you enter, stay there, and from there depart. And whoever will not receive you, when you go out of that city, shake off the very dust from your feet as testimony against them.'*" *(Luke 9:3-5)*

God is actively involved and intimately interested in our wholeness, even down to the number of hairs on our head. Jesus encouraged the disciples to depend on Him, not to be careless in preparation. The symbol of 'shaking the dust from their feet' was to be used by the disciples whenever their message was rejected. It was to remind them that those who rejected Jesus and the principles He stood for were cut off from God's people and under His judgment.

"but the very hairs on your head are all numbered. Do not fear, therefore; you are of more value than many sparrows."
(Luke 12:7)

Christ is saying, "Let everything rest on me. Let our relationship be your balancing point."[19] Looking at a new perspective, the world is turned upside down and our lives are balanced on Him and not on our self-sufficiency. As a Christian, one believes that Christ is actively and intimately involved in the needs and concerns of daily life. Satisfaction of all needs is met through God's regeneration of soil, sun, water, and air; it is God that gives the spark of life and it is Christ who offers eternal love and heavenly value.

Generation upon generation learns mores and cultural lessons that sustain the next to come. Assessing spiritual values is easily observed by God's love as the true 'child of God' beams outward to others in his or her presence. "Unless we reclaim our inner child, we have no inner sense of self and gradually the imposter becomes who we really think we are"[18]

SUMMARY
CHAPTER TWO - CHILD OF GOD

It was you, God, who *"fashioned me in my mother's womb."* *(Psalm 139:13)* Perfection in the plan could only come from Our Creator, God. The Bible clearly spells out God's intention for the healthy maintenance of all people. Scriptures from the Books of Leviticus and Deuteronomy are cited regarding health ordinances and laws.

Infants are born "ready"—ready to learn, ready to explore and ready to begin the earthly sequence of "taking in" what we developmentally are capable of learning. The Brazelton Neonatal Assessment Index describes an infant's competencies and individuality, measuring 18 behavior and reflex items, designed to examine the newborn's physiological, motor state, and social capacities. Maslow's Hierarchy of needs, Piaget's cognitive development and Carl Jung's theory of personality and spirituality all deal with motivational needs and their sequencing.

There is wholeness and completeness in our very introduction to the family unit, and more importantly, wholeness and completeness in the community of God's people. Our bodies are living temples of the Holy Spirit. Stewardship of this God-given treasure requires knowledge, instruction and reason.

My dear friend, whose wit and wisdom comforted me time and again with a constant thread of God's love, was made real to me as she expressed each experience transitioning from child to mother to grandmother, then great grandmother. She clearly understood God's kingdom and our role as mentors for future generations. What are spiritual values and how are they translated? Do we develop spiritual sensitivity over time? How can future generations benefit from our struggles?

QUESTIONS
CHAPTER TWO - CHILD OF GOD

1. Define *Biblical Wholeness* as it relates to healing for each individual. How does that differ from "Biblical Wholeness" in the community of believers?

2. Identify four different theories of learning. Give an example of how each spoke to your learning patterns in life.

3. Prove/disprove Maslow's Hierarchy of Needs based on your experiences. How will your patient care be changed with what you learned?

4. What is spiritual sensitivity? What key concepts are needed for me to change?

5. What responsibility do we have for teaching spirituality to future generations?

RESOURCES

1. Bergman Ronald et al., *Atlas of Microscopic Anatomy:* Section 13: Female reproductive System.

2. Harvard Medical School (2005). *The Brazelton Institue,* "The Newborn Behavioral Observation System: What is it?" http://www.brazelton-institute.com/clnbas.html

3. Piaget, jean, Internet Resource, 2006.

4. Simons, Janet, Donald Irwin and Beverly Drinnien, (1987). *Psychology: the Search for Understanding,* New York: West Publishing Company.

5. Boeree, C. George, the *Journal of Humanistic Psychology,* July 1998

6. Kraybill, Donald, the *Upside Down Kingdom,* Scottsdale: Herald Press, 1990

7. Jung, Carl, http://en.wikipedia.org/wiki/Carl_Jung

8. Ibid

9. Ibid

10. Internet resource, *Food in Biblical Times,* Page 165

11. Marill, Marcia, *Experiencing Biblical Wholeness,* Columbus: Brentwood Christian Press, Page 143

12. Vos, Howard (1999), *Bible Manners and customs,* Nashville: Thomas Nelson Publishers, Incorporated. Page 484

13. Food in Biblical Times. Page 165

14. Food in Biblical Times. Page 165

15. Vos, Howard, *Bible Manners and Customs,* Nashville: Thomas Nelson, 1999. Page 484

16. Marill, Marcia, *Experiencing Biblical Wholeness*, Columbus: Brentwood Christian Press. Page 143

17. Ibid, Page 145

18. Kraybill, Donald, *The Upside Down Kingdom*, Scottsdale: Herald Press, 1990

19. Brennan, Manning, *Abba's Child*, Colorado Springs: Navpress Books and Bible Studies, 1994. pages 96-97

CHAPTER THREE
HOW LOVING AM I?

The heavy metal prison door slammed shut—clanggg! I hurriedly looked at the guards to reassure myself that everything was okay or normal, if you can call a prison setting normal. In the early spring of 1997, I joined a group of volunteers from our church district to visit women in prison. I recall the anticipation that I felt as the time drew near. I wanted so much to help those in need but little did I know what God had in store for me. To this day, the lessons continue to reap rewards tenfold.

In every generation, there is probably no word that is translated more, sung about more or experienced more than love. God is love. It is in God's image that we are created, nurtured, sculpted and transformed. The Greek words, *eros* (physical, sexual intimacy between man and wife), *agape* (the highest form of love, charity...love of God for man and man for God) and *phileo* (brotherly love)[1] point out the different forms that love takes. Love is understood in the Old Testament primarily in terms of the covenant relationship between God and Israel. The English word "love" is built on the Old Testament foundation. The New Testament describes a love built on that foundation but able to overcome a hostile environment. Again and again, God's steadfast love for Israel (hesed) is shown by His faithfulness to the covenant. *"And for their sake He remembered His covenant; and relented according to the multitude of His mercies." (Psalm 106:45),* one side being God's care of Israel, the other, Israel's faithful response.

"During the Middle Ages, love and good works were viewed as being part of the gospel. A person's love was shown by their obedience to the law."[1] It is also used to indicate the 'romantic relationship' of a boy and girl. Love means one person's desire of another and the satisfaction of being with that person. Eric Fromm (1900-1980), internationally renowned German-American psychologist and humanistic philosopher, understands love as an art.[2] He also believes that love is the overcoming of separation, of man fearing union for one reason—namely, that he will lose his own individuality.

Paul Tillich in *Love, Power and Justice,* defines Christian love as that which unites life. Man is drawn toward physical pleasure for its own sake (eros.) He is drawn toward the beautiful, which he encounters in many forms (libido.) He is drawn toward people because he sees union with them as the fulfillment of himself (philos).[3] In his book, *Amazing Grace: 366 Hymn Stories for Daily Devotions,* Kenneth Osbeck states that "we must never underestimate the power of love in our human relationships-- whether marriage, family, business associations or friendships. The divine love of God for man far exceeds all other forms of love."[4] Man is drawn out of his self-centered preferences as the basis for union with others when he comes to know that he and other people ultimately belong to the same Creator. Thus all men belong to the same creative process and find fulfillment in working together in this one process. Out of this sense of belonging, man is united with all that is, or "agape" love. In agape, all estrangement is overcome by the reunion of the whole. God-like love is so much more expansive than we humans can imagine. It is literally "wide open", as with amazement and wonder.

That day of my visit to the prison, all assigned volunteers were prepared with the agenda of the day, ten hours spent with female inmates in a protected setting, in this case, a gymnasium rearranged into a makeshift conference room. We were to sit with the women at round tables of six, forming small study groups. Led by guards, the women were chaperoned into the meeting room in a single file. My heart went out to them as I saw their glances, some looking directly at me and some looking away as though they didn't want to be recognized. We greeted them en masse and were then divided into small groups. When I saw the nametag of Rachel, my assigned prison contact, I couldn't believe my eyes. If I had a twin, she couldn't have looked more like me. I swallowed hard and immediately thought, "Who is going to help who here? That could be me!" But there, for the grace of God, go I. Our assignment was to share with each other a hurtful situation of our past. I chose a safe subject, my failed business venture following retirement, taking care to keep the conversation non-judgmental while we shared feelings and experiences. Rachel looked relieved to have a day away from her usual routine. She delivered a talk that I wish I could have taped.

Rachel's story revealed hatred; hatred from the onset of her tenure at the prison with hatred continuing on a daily basis. I heard of practices that were not human, of women required to don protective equipment as the sound of a horn signaled the release of attack dogs. The dogs pursued her until she climbed a tree, if there was time. This story and the series of events that took place among the fifteen "women in white" taught a world of lessons to me and the rest of the volunteers. More than anything else, it reminded me of the lessons that Christ was sent to teach us.

"Love the Lord your God with all your heart." (Matthew 22:37) Jesus asks for total devotion from His disciples. John Wesley, founder of Methodism, saw Christian perfection in this love. God alone is the source of genuine and unconditional love that can be continually poured into us; it can then flow to others in the natural outpouring or sharing of that love. According to scripture, God never changes in God's expectations. *"If you love me, you will keep my commandments." (John 14:15)* Genuine love for Jesus results in genuine surrender of my will to God's greater will. Individuals who choose to follow Jesus are gradually released from purposes contrary to the will of God. Until that happens, the lessons will be repeated over and over again.

Each time I drift off course and find myself out of balance, I find help from the First Book of Corinthians..."Love is patient; love is kind" (1 Corinthians 13:4) urging me to be patient with other peoples' mistakes. When I found myself being impatient with a situation or a person, I rested in the fact that *"Love never ends" (1 Corinthians 13:8)*. The delicate balance of body - mind - spirit is challenged constantly. What did it mean, *"to be rooted and grounded in love? (Ephesians 3:17) to be strengthened by the spirit, to have the indwelling Christ, and to be established in love?* These are basic to Christian growth. The fullness of this love, *"to know the love of Christ" (Ephesians 3:19)* passes our human knowledge, though we may know in experiences what we cannot explain intellectually.

John 4:12 tells us that *"God lives in us, and this love is perfected in us."* God reaches His goal for us when love controls our thoughts and actions. Perfect love, made possible by the indwelling Holy Spirit is both the Christian's primary obligation and his highest privilege. Who is the recipient of this love? It is each of us and all those with whom we come in contact. We are tested daily, sometimes hourly it seems, to grow in grace and to reach out to others who need God's love. We mature spiritually only with support and caring from those who *"speak the truth in love" (Ephesians 4:15).* Hearts established in the Christian faith encourage one another and are united in love.

> *"...that their hearts may be encouraged being knit together in love and attaining to all riches of the full assurance of understanding, to the knowledge of the mystery of God, both of the Father and of Christ," (Colossians 2:2).*

God taught me that being united in love with the community of believers brought me into full knowledge of revealed truth.

When I feel the need for protection, I am in tune with my vulnerability and I am longing for God to shield me with love. Belief in God's Word arms me with faith, love and the hope against negative emotions that prevent me from feeling compassion toward others. I must envision *"putting on the breastplate of faith and love" (1 Thessalonians 5:8).* The greatest gift I ever gave my patients came with the realization that that *"there is no fear in love" (John 4:12).* Perfect love casts out fear, allowing us to rest in God and freely give of ourselves to others. In their book on healing prayer, Tilda Norberg and Robert Webber describe the pursuit of our call to wholeness. "Because the Holy Spirit is continually at work pushing each of us toward wholeness, the process of healing is like removing sticks and leaves from a stream until the water runs clear. If we simply get out of the way of the Lord's work in us, we can trust that we are being led to the particular kind of wholeness God wills for us."[5]

There is always something that we can give to another person that spells out hope, encouragement, guidance, solace or physical help. There is joy and fulfillment in living out God's purpose, whether others receive it in the spirit it was given or not. Through healing prayer, we discern God's will and surrender to the healing journey as it unfolds in us. This healing journey teaches us to find the gift that our suffering and brokenness offer.[6] What better way can there be for one person to help another! God reaches the goal for us when love controls our thoughts and actions. Perfect love, made possible by allowing the Holy Spirit to dwell and operate in us is both the Christian's primary obligation and his highest privilege. John 4:19 states: *"We love because he first loved us."* Perfect love for God transforms our relationship to God to others.

We all have our prisons, internal or external. We all share hopes, dreams and sorrows, regardless of our beginnings. Didn't these women deserve God's love as much as any other? How was God at work here? What was God teaching me? Could the avenue suited to my gifts and calling be realized better here than in a hospital setting? Needless to say, I left the entry gates of the prison that day with a new appreciation for every aspect of life. If one word were uppermost in my thoughts and prayers as I relived the trip, it would be "hope". At times, hope may be all that seems tangible, even though it sometimes takes a stretch to pull that hope into view. "Belief" in a different possibility is the glimmer that I see as a nurse's very being.

Love tempers our attitude. As God kneads our hearts and reveals new understanding, anger, rage, malice, slander or lying will no longer be necessary. Attitudes reveal to other people our true countenance. It takes discipline to evaluate our everyday communication but it is a must if we are to serve the Lord. First, God helps us to no longer give way to anger or rage in the form of temper tantrums, or any violent display or attack by either word or deed upon another person. When the 'old self' tempts us, old habits no longer have power over us. We can say "no" because we are transformed in heart and mind by God's Spirit. We become literally *"new creatures in Christ" (Galatians 5:17).*

Love is about reaching beyond us to someone else and continuing to work with a newfound happiness that causes us to pause, look and learn from our past. It is much too easy to blame others for our weaknesses or make excuses for our behavior based on the newest theory or justification for what we know to be wrong. The Book of Matthew says this very clearly,

"And why do you look at the speck in your brother's eye but do not consider the plank in your own eye?" (Matthew 7:3)

SUMMARY
CHAPTER THREE - HOW LOVING AM I?

A visit to a prison provided lessons well beyond my expectation. The power of love has not changed throughout the generations. Three Greek words describe the different forms that love takes-- *agape, eros* and *phileo*. Love in the past and the present day is shown by obedience to God's law. Man is drawn out of his self-centeredness when he realizes that he and other men, ultimately belong to the same Creator.

Agape love is effusive; it is beyond anyone's expectation; it is unconditional. *"Love the lord your God with all your heart" (Matthew 22:37).* Jesus asks for total devotion. God alone is the source of genuine and unconditional love continually poured out on us.

Genuine love for Jesus results in genuine surrender of my will to God's greater will. Until I am aware of the lessons presented for learning, I may repeat the same scenarios continuously. God reaches His goal for us when true love controls our thoughts and actions. An analogy on cleansing of our inner selves and clearing of sticks and leaves from a stream gives a visual map of health.

QUESTIONS
CHAPTER THREE - HOW LOVING AM I?

1. Name three Greek words that describe different forms of love. Elaborate on their differences.

2. If God alone is the source of genuine and unconditional love, why do we often feel fulfilled by our human contacts?

3. Cleansing of the inner self requires dedicated, applied precepts. Describe a circumstance that in your life had new meaning once the clutter was removed.

4. Project in your own mind, life in a prison. What examples would you share of God's love and care of every single human being on earth.

RESOURCES

1. Strong, James (2015) *Strong's Expanded Concordance.* https://amazon.com/Strong's Concordance.

2. Fromm, Eric, *Definitions of Love: Christian Word Book,* Nashville: Methodist Publishing House, 1968. Page 182

3. Ibid, Page 183

4. Osbeck, Kenneth, (2002), *Amazing Grace: 366 Hymn Stories.* Grand Rapids: Kregel Publishers

5. Norberg, Tilda and Robert Webber, *Stretch Out Your Hand: Exploring Healing Prayer,* Nashville: Upper Room Books, 1998. Page 58

CHAPTER FOUR
GOD'S VIEW: MY POTENTIAL

God's plan for each and every one of us involves relationship with the Almighty. Unless and until that relationship is born, nourished and matures, we struggle at the human level of existence, not associated with a dynamic future and not in time with the wisdom that awaits God's children as truth is revealed. In this chapter, I recall the funeral of Katie; yes, Grandma Katie of Chapter Two whose wisdom, wit, knowledge and love of the Lord catapulted my learning to heights I never dreamed.

I entered the pew in my home church where I saw two friends from a Bible Study class. Then a spirit of loneliness hit me like a ton of bricks--my friend was about to be buried, my friend who had changed my life in the course of the last five years. A joyful mother of four, her positive countenance endeared her to me from our very first meeting. When I think of love, I think of Katie and the depth of her spirituality. We shared our life journeys and growing appreciation for God's work in our lives.

From the greatness of God and the majesty of creation to the microscopic reality of God, it was all in The Creator's hands. My friends and I stood to sing the Hymn of Promise. Consider these words:

Hymn of Promise
United Methodist Hymnal

Verse 1

In the bulb there is a flower, in the seed, an apple tree;

In cocoons a hidden promise: butterflies will soon be free.

In the cold and snow of winter, there's a spring that waits to be;

Unrevealed until its season, something God alone can see.

Verse 2

There's a song in every silence, seeking word and melody;

There's a dawn in every darkness, bringing hope for you and me.

From the past will come the future; what it holds, a mystery,

Unrevealed until its season, something God alone can see.

Verse 3

In our end is our beginning; in our time, infinity;

In our doubt there is believing; in our life, eternity.

In our death, a resurrection; at the last, a victory,

Unrevealed until its season, something God alone can see.

Reassurance and comfort enveloped me. As stated in the hymn, there awaits in each dormant seed the potential for future growth, whether it is a plant, animal or human being. Because God is the only force that causes growth, I believe our role is absolutely within our grasp and more clear-cut than we can imagine. Jesus loved nature. His parables spoke to topics that people of the day could understand. They still speak to us today. I believe God intended it to be that way. Our holistic potential includes relationships. Because our gifts and talents are so much a part of who we are, the way we translate God's love to others will be just as unique. God's love is the fulfillment of the law; when we are perfected in love, we have been perfected in all. Our actions will reveal the choice we have made.

"These are the things you shall do: Speak each man the truth to his neighbor. Give judgment in your gates for truth, justice and peace." (Zechariah 8:16)

In keeping with Biblical statutes and promises, we are given land, family and rule over each of these in the Master's plan. For every possible route, there is a reaffirmation of God's law. A balance exists between nature and man. The Law of Torah states that land must rest every seven years. Of the sevens days of the week, we are admonished to enjoy the day of rest for the Sabbath.

The key is for each of us to reach out to God for guidance, clarity and vision and to then connect with our neighbor. That neighbor may be the physical neighbor next door, the neighborhood of the community or the neighborhood of the world. Reaching out begins with connections. Those connections begin in the home where we learn to reach beyond ourselves to our neighbors. The face of the neighbor changes as our peer group changes, becoming our work group, our study group and our support group. Eventually, we realize how small the world really is, and our neighbor is one we meet on a mission trip in other parts of the world. God created each and every one of us, *"for such a time as this."* *(Esther 4:4)* I believe that God's Word encompasses positive choices that lead to those connections. It is as simple as believing the best in nature and people, and trusting that all growth is done with an eye to heaven.

Webster's dictionary defines *potential* as "what can be, but as yet, is not; with a possibility or likelihood of occurring, or of doing or becoming something in the future."[2] My earliest memories are centered on Mom and the purring of the sewing machine. I can remember sitting on a blanket at her feet while she sang to me and encouraged me to "make something for yourself with this material." In fact, I still have the first coin purse I made at age three. Mom knew many stories, shared songs of life and answered all my questions. As I grew to understand more, she always, always left the discussion of my future with the same advice. "Just remember, Donna, there is nothing in this world that you can't do if you put your mind to it!" Well, I believed her. Is it any wonder that two of my childhood favorites were Mighty Mouse and The Little Engine That Could?

In school, I remember the most significant change taking place in the fourth and fifth grade. My fourth grade teacher saw something in me that needed very little encouragement, and she enabled that growth through educational challenges. If I completed assignments before the class, she had me creating an extra credit project. I can remember asking more questions on one day than ever before. The experience was like a light bulb being turned on. I suddenly had increased energy, thought of ways to express the project, book or story, and rallied the other students to take part in the upcoming report. Every time I learned the answer to one of the questions, the next popped up within seconds. I felt like a sponge as I soaked in all new knowledge at every threshold of learning.

God's promises are repeated in the books of the Holy Bible. Whether we look historically at the promises fulfilled or believe through faith that we will be provided for, it takes a stretch beyond our comfort zone to remember that God's truths will carry us through. A truth in one section of the Bible will not be disconnected in another. Yes, there are gaps of time, but not gaps in meaning.

Meister Eckhart, the fourteenth century German mystic was best know for his creation theology. He was strongly influenced by the Holy Bible and Jewish thinking. He asserted that to understand a man's theology is to realize how he relates to his universe. Eckhart joined the Dominican Order during this fifteenth to seventeenth year where he remained for fifty-three years. This order was specifically for friars actively involved in the world--the world of universities, towns and cities. Meister Eckhart witnesses to his total dependence on Scripture. He said, "I believe more in Scripture than I do in myself. The Holy Scripture is like the sea it is so deep. No one is so wise that if he wished to probe it, he would not find something more and deeper in it."[4] Thomas Aquinas was also a protégé and was associated with the Dominican Spiritual movement. They found divinity reflected in nature, in and around them-the mountains, stones, trees, lakes, springs, the sea and every type of animal.

The cycle of life portrayed by the *Hymn of Promise* clearly spells out the mystery of God's creation. In the first verse, the bulb, the seed and the cocoon all completely house the future plant or insect that awaits birthing. During the "hidden time,"

God is sculpting perfection. Seasons of the year spill one into the next, and as the song says, God's truths remain unrevealed until the season that God has planned. The second verse speaks of contrasts: song--silence, word--melody, past--future, mystery--revelation. Opposites of end--beginning, our time--infinity (God's time), our death--victorious resurrection, unrevealed until its season, reassuring us that in God's time all will be revealed.

Reinforcement of positive behaviors is the key motivator that will inspire a child. Our "potential" is most seen by those who live with us and observe our everyday behaviors. One way of understanding our gifts, strengths and talents is through a study of our spiritual gifts. As a child, we rely on feedback from our parents, family and caretakers.

> *"having then gifts differing according to the grace that is given to us, let us use them: if prophecy, let us prophecy in proportion to our faith; or ministry, let us use it in our ministering; he who teaches, in teaching; he who exhorts in exhortation; he who gives, with liberality; he who leads, with diligence, he who shows mercy, with cheerfulness."* (Romans 12:6-8)

The impact was life changing as I learned of my own spiritual gifts. I reviewed my personal strengths on the Birkman Assessment Tool[3] which measures ministry strengths in four categories:

1. Leadership - Wisdom, Apostleship, Shepherding
2. Visioning - Creative Communication, Teaching, Mercy, Encouragement Healing/Intercession
3. Communication - Evangelism, Exhortation, Hospitality, Discernment, Prophecy

4. Service - Craftsmanship, Security/Enforcement, Maintenance/Operations, Technology/Computer, Systems/Science

My individual results confirmed areas that were a "natural" for me - wisdom (Leadership) teaching mercy and encouragement (Visioning) and extremely high in evangelism, exhortation, hospitality, discernment (Communication) and Service. I pondered the results and thanked God for the breadth of talents with which I was blessed.

I then administered the questionnaire to twenty parish nurses. After completing their questionnaires and taking averages, the scores of the nurses were almost a mirror image of mine and also of the vocation they chose. In sharing this information on spiritual gifts at church and with my nursing peers, I found the same enthusiasm in almost everyone as they discovered their strengths. Later, in my capacity of assigning parish nurses to serve in various churches, I felt reassured that each of them would produce stellar results. It is crucial to every individual's potential to gain even a cursory understanding of the gifts they were granted at birth. Even a cursory understanding of the gifts is a requirement to understand your passions and talents. When we operate in our best self as a natural state, we are providing God an opportunity for reaching each person's heart with whom we come in contact.

Generation upon generation journeys in the world acculturated to believe the teachings of that time and place. As God's Word is shared, refreshing new insights take place. Our relationship with God grows and takes on individual meaning for us in the very location and vocation we find ourselves. When did I learn that I had potential? I think I always knew it. What hidden promises from God do you possess?

SUMMARY
CHAPTER FOUR - GOD'S VIEW - MY POTENTIAL

God's master design included me well before I was born. Because God reveals truth in stages, I must constantly remind myself to *"set your mind on things above, not on things in the earth."* *(Colossians 3:2)* To be a creature of God holds an expectation, an unrealized fulfillment that can only be satisfied by God. God is every bit good and desires our central focus to be heavenward as we learn our heavenly potential. I believe that God's view of me is my human potential fully realized. What would that look like? I envisioned a balance of body, mind and spirit as peace began to be revealed in my behavior and body language.

Of all the senses -- hearing, sight, touch, smell and taste, the two that seem to become immediately permeable to evil are sight and hearing. Do I believe what I see and hear? The well-developed sense of hearing is begun in utero as the baby listens to Mama's heartbeat. The soothing, repetitive drum-like beat reminds the infant of his or her one-ness with mother. This keen sense follows him into the world as he follows the sounds, smell, touch and sight of Mama. Nurturing Mother is the one identity to which the baby clings. I liken the magnetic draw to my own mother just as I do to God.

Meister Eckhart's terms:

When I preach, I am accustomed to speak about detachment, and that man should be free of himself and of all things; second, that man should be formed again into that simple good which is God; third, that he should reflect on the great nobility with which God has endowed his soul, so that in this way he may come again to wonder at God; fourth, about the purity of the divine nature for the brightness of the divine nature is beyond words. God is a word -- a word unspoken.

Potential represents possibility. *"For the promise is for you and your children..." (Acts 2:39)* God's promises helped give me a vision of the goal, a vision of the future. When I set my sights on heaven, I relinquish my hold on the outcome of the day and release it to heaven's plan.

QUESTIONS
CHAPTER FOUR - GOD'S VIEW - MY POTENTIAL

1. What does a "heavenward" focus mean to you? List three specific incidents when you looked to human understanding instead of praying to God for an answer.

2. Do you agree or disagree that sight and hearing are the two senses most often involved in the recognition of "evil"? Defend your position.

3. Meister Eckhart's sermon addresses four key areas. What does he mean that man can:

a. Be free of himself and all things? (Detachment)

b. Be formed again into a simple good? (Transformation)

c. Reflect on his soul's nobility? (Appreciation)

d. Consider his divine nature? (Contemplating our destiny)

4. God's promises are for us as well as our children. List two of God's promises that you have seen answered in your lifetime.

RESOURCES

1. Hymn of Promise #707, *United Methodist Hymnal.* Nashville:United Methodist Publishing, (1989)

2. Internet Dictionary, http://dictionary.reference.com/ potential

3. Birkman Assessment Tool, Advanced Report. (1994), Houston: Birkman International, Inc.

4. Eckhart, Meister (1986), *Meister Eckhart Teacher and Preacher,* The Classics of Western Spirituality. New York: Paulist Press

CHAPTER FIVE
A COVENANT BOND

I sank into the leather chair at the counselor's office--too weak to fight and too unsure of what my responses would be. At least my husband agreed to come with me. My plan had fallen apart. I thought that retirement was a natural, easy follow-on to a successful career in the Air Force. Yet with the business failure, my pride took the greatest hit. I hadn't counted on God for much up until this point, but I sure needed direction now. At first I didn't understand that I was still trying to "prove myself," but put in the context of an unexpected failure, I wasn't sure where I stood in my husband's eyes. Would he think less of me? Would he be angry? Would I be put down every time the subject came up? I was lost, ashamed and lonely. I began to feel really lost. What was my role now and how could I find my way? I couldn't relax. I was still driven. My heart raced every time the thoughts of customers not paying...the court dates...the unpaid debt. Over and over, I just wanted to run. I buried myself in projects. I shopped when I felt sad and I exercised well beyond my body's ideal limit. Still, no relief was in sight. All I wanted to do was to get well. The only sure thing that I knew was that my weekly counseling appointment afforded a time to relay the trials to someone who would not judge, not reprimand and not accuse. I was numb with grief. How do I deal with this loss?

My husband has just come home from his normal twenty day/month flying schedule and was totally frustrated with my business failure. He had every right to be frustrated; after all, I was $33,000 in debt. The worst part was that I was not sure how I let it all happen, but when the stress caused my increased moodiness, my inability to concentrate, poor driving, and constant tear-eyed demeanor, I knew it was time to ask him to accompany me to the counselor's office. All I saw that day was "failure...failure...failure" in big bright letters. The eternal optimist, I continued to see the negatives all turning to successes. I wanted my version of success to be the result. After all, I still wanted control. Success was not what I felt at that moment, in fact, success wasn't any part of who or where I was. Even being in that situation, I could still imagine the negatives each turning into successes.

If the "Covenant of Marriage" holds true, and I know God never rescinds promises, I asked myself how I was to get from this point to a workable solution that would save our marriage. I didn't want to admit that I had made a mistake; after all, that was the first real failure I had ever experienced. Little did I know how God would use every bit of my disappointment to educate me in the ways of the world. Why was I still trying to prove myself? Where had I gone wrong? Dear Lord, please help me see the Donna that you created me to be.

My Biblical search for the meaning of "Covenant" started in the Book of Genesis. Two types of covenants existed - theological and political. Covenants repeat over and over the solid nature of God's promises. I looked at nature and remembered God's promises to the people. One well-known vow made by God is highlighted in the Book of Genesis: *"I set my rainbow in the cloud and it shall be for the sign of the covenant between Me and the earth." (Genesis 9:13)*

God honors each and every covenant that is made. Since this remains true, I trusted that God was and is with me through anything that could possibly happen to me here on earth. I will trust in that and put Him at the center of my thought, words and actions. A Godly solution, I believe, can take place.

A covenant bond was a contract in the ancient world. Today, it is a binding and solemn agreement by two or more parties to do or to keep from doing something specified. In the original covenant between God and man, the Abrahamic Covenant, God promised to make of him a great nation and to bless all generations of families given to his governance. The Davidic Covenant, declaring him a royal family, explains the means through which the earlier promises to Abraham would be fulfilled. The New Covenant described in the Book of Jeremiah reinforces the Abrahamic as well as the Davidic promises. These elements include the Davidic line through which the covenant fulfillment is realized, the New Covenant made with Israel, involving individual and national conversion, and projects the time of universal knowledge of the Lord.

"Because God wanted to make the unchanging nature of His purpose very clear to the heirs of what was promised, He confirmed it with an oath.[1] Abraham's contract with God was unconditional. God bound Himself to make the unchanging nature of His purpose very clear, *"I will establish your line forever and make your throne firm through all generations."* *(Psalm 39:3-4).* In *My Utmost for His Highest,* Oswald Chamber states: "Man must go beyond the physical body and feelings in his covenant with God, just as God goes beyond himself in reaching out with the covenant to man. We tend to have faith in our feelings. In other words, I don't believe God until I have something tangible in my hand, so that I know I have it."[2]

As I matured and considered a mate for my life's journey, I remember taking a long time to evaluate not only my feelings, but to learn of my then fiancée's integrity and active commitment to similar life goals. Covenant responsibility weighed heavy on my heart. After all, a marriage is not only about a one-time commitment but a legal partnership that is binding until death.

> *"Now to the married I command, yet not I but the Lord: a wife is not to depart from her husband. But even if she does depart, let her remain unmarried or be reconciled to her husband. And a husband is not divorce his wife."* *(1 Corinthians 7:10-11)*

The marriage covenant carries with it expectations and obligations, the expectation of caring and honesty seemed automatically understood, but I vividly remember observing my fiancée's responses to everyday situations, to stressful situations, to illness and to emergency situations.

Obligations of each party became particularly significant as these three areas were discussed--decision-making, mutual understanding and legal matters. Who in the relationship would be making the decisions? How will differing opinions be resolved? What about a family? What strengths do each of us possess?

Family covenants hold with them an obligation to meet the needs of those concerned--physical needs, educational needs and spiritual needs. As tenets for a solid marriage, the discussion of these issues is critical. Regarding child rearing, primary care giving and handling of problems in varied scenarios all mattered. Where did I fit into the picture and how had I responded as a covenant partner?

The seeds of Messiah's teachings are found in the prophecies of Hebrew Scriptures, the Old Testament. Many Old Testament lessons have direct application to contemporary nursing practice, one important concept for today's nurses is that of the nurse/patient *covenant*.[3] This interpretation relates specifically to the important dimension of trust occurring between nurses and their patients. Although not always formally articulated as such the presence of an understood covenant between a patient and nurse not only supports the concepts of trust between the partners, but also sets up parameters for appropriate role behaviors and attitudes.

And if either of us breaks a vow, how will we go about forgiving one another? When the foundation of trust has been broken, three components of healing include: 1) genuine repentance. 2) humility and 3) proof of a changed life. Regarding repentance, Ezekiel 33:15 states

> *"if the wicked restores the pledge, gives back what he has stolen and walks in the statues of life without committing iniquity, he shall surely live; he shall not die in this life, there is no unpardonable sin for the person who truly repents."*

In this life, there is always pardon from God.

> *"Because your heart was tender and you humbled yourself before God when you heard His words against this place*

and against its inhabitants and you humbled yourself before me, and you tore your clothes and wept before Me, I also have heard you, says the Lord." (2 Chronicles 34:27)

Proof of a changed life will be apparent as new behaviors replace the old.

"But someone will say, 'you have faith, and I have works.' Show me your faith without your works, and I will show you my faith by my works." (James 2:18)

"Faith without works, is no better than words without deeds." (James 2:15-17)

"Faith can be neither seen nor verified unless it shows itself in works." (James 2:18)

It is not easy to forgive as God forgives, but it is as essential for the one wronged as for the one needing forgiveness. Two main stumbling blocks are anger and lack of forgiveness. When we are angry, the focus is on self and feelings. It is much better to be angry at the sin and the destruction it causes. Judgment about the results of a person's wrongdoing is for God alone. We are commanded to forgive.

"And be kind to one another, forgiving of one another, even as God in Christ forgave you." (Ephesians 4:32)

Forgiveness is learned. "True forgiveness is to see through the eyes of Mercy to the real person created in the likeness of God, to cease seeing the offense of the man and to send it away from him, by not attributing it to his account."[4] As we learn to forgive others and leave the "justice" up to God, we are forgiven our sins as well. Judgment about the person guilty of wrongdoing is for God alone. When anger escalates to rage or any violent display or attack, by either word or deed upon one another, we must remember that it is no longer acceptable to escalate to rage... say no to harboring bitterness because we are new creatures in Christ, completely forgiven. Renouncing attitudes of malice, slander, filthy language and lying will leave room for us to be filled with the light and be self-controlled.

SUMMARY
CHAPTER FIVE - A COVENANT BOND

At last, my husband agreed to come to counseling with me. My pride kept me from coming any sooner. After all, he had a right to be upset. I had experienced a business failure...and incurred a debt of $33,000. The worst part was that I didn't know how it had happened. Obviously, I should have listened to those who counseled me to choose something closer to what I used to do. Now, I had to count on God because I had traveled way beyond my learning.

My biblical search for the meaning of covenant revolved around God's initial covenant with Abraham. With that as a base, the two areas that came to light were the theological covenants of marriage and family relationships. The basis of covenant relationships has to be trust. Trust and commitment work together to yield perseverance in any and all situations. Selfish as we humans are, it is often hard to move beyond our comfort zones in making real progress. Trust encompasses character, a history of integrity and a rebuilding of trust if it has been broken. Covenants repeat over and over the eternal promises of God. I looked at nature and immediately appreciated the Creator's touch.

As I struggled with the pieces I had to examine, I realized that both my husband and I had come to the marriage with certain expectations. Up until the business challenge, I generally reached my goals. In the marriage covenant, expectations translated into obligations, three of which were decision-making, mutual understanding and legal matters. We now trusted each other to pour out our hearts and look at all the facts. Fortunately for me, my husband knew where the financial problems were and I had to figure a way to make the needed changes over time. I learned a lot about anger and forgiveness that day. What I expected and feared never happened. The worst-case scenario was already in the past and I thanked God for the miracles in our marriage. I remembered that I could only be perfected in love if I forgave myself. Behavior change was needed and I now had manageable steps. The keys to positive relationships rang true again. If communication lines are kept open, there is nothing that cannot be handled in a marriage--with the help of God and with the other partner.

QUESTIONS
CHAPTER FIVE - A COVENANT BOND

1. Covenant relationships encompass two major agreements in our culture and society. What union is tested by each one and how will danger areas be noticed?

2. The foundation of trust and commitment are basic to understanding God's promises. How will I know if trust has been broken?

3. God sanctions theological covenants. What physical sign did God first leave to remind us that he would never again flood the earth?

4. Behaviors contrary to the covenant may sabotage relationships. How important is it to evaluate the changes together as opposed to individually?

RESOURCES

1. Richards, L. (1987), *The Teacher's Commentary*, Wheaton: Scripture Press. Page 48

2. Chambers, Oswald (1992), *My Utmost for His Highest Devotional Journal*, Grand Rapids: Discovery House Publishers, December 6th

3. Sawatsky, Rick and Barbara Pesut, (2005) Journal of Holistic Nursing *Trinity Western University: Attributes of Spiritual Care in Nursing Practice*, Page 25S

4. O'Donnell, Michele (2005), *The God We Have Created*, San Antonio: La Vida Press. Page 217

CHAPTER SIX
PERCEPTION IS 100%

Nursing is unique in its grounding. It is said that one foot is in the sciences and one in religion. I attribute that to the body-mind-spirit balance that brings us to the peak of our practice, when we are in the groove, doing what we love and knowing that we have positively influenced our patients. How is my nursing vocation the conduit for God's healing touch? How is my unique 'presence' a stretch of God's hand to His hurting children? I pondered the depth of my perception and thought about God's Scriptures related to children and how Jesus' interactions with children turned into life-long lessons for adults.

Scriptures whirled in my mind. How did my childhood experiences affect my adult understanding?

"People were bringing little children to Him in order that He might touch them and the disciples spoke sternly to

them. But when Jesus saw this, He was indignant and said to them, "Let the little children come to Me; do not stop them; for it is to such as these that the Kingdom of God belongs. Truly I tell you, whoever does not receive the kingdom of God as a little child will never enter it. And He took them up in His arms, laid His hands on them and blessed them." (Mark 10:13-16)

How I remember being open to the beauty of others when I was a child. I had no pre-conceived ideas of how they should think, act or be. How refreshing to return to Jesus' words of wisdom, not blaming the inexperience of youth but rejoicing in its freshness.

"If any of you put a stumbling block before one of these little ones who believes is Me, it would be better for you if a great millstone were fastened around your neck and you were drowned in the depth of the sea. Woe to the world because of stumbling blocks! Occasions for stumbling are bound to come but woe to the one by whom the stumbling block comes!" (Matthew 17:6-7)

The power of this message hit home since I had watched so many held back from learning of Jesus. We do the same today—block true learning about the greatest messages to those in all stages of the faith journey. We who know Jesus' intent, know to shepherd others to answers. We must not block the learning, beginning with the very attitudes of our youth.

"When I was a child, I spoke like a child, I thought like a child, I reasoned like a child; when I became an adult, I put an end to childish ways." (1 Corinthians 13:11)

When I think of a child, I think of their purity of spirit. They are open in their perception (taking in all that surrounds them) and single-minded in their focus. Because they are single minded and in a sense, uncluttered by the world's influence, they are able to focus clearly on one thing at a time. Be a child as you read these treasured words of the Beatitudes. Savor God's rich intent by really hearing Matthew's telling of the story.

THE BEATITUDES

First

"Blessed are the poor in spirit, for theirs is the kingdom of heaven." (Matthew 5:3)

The first Beatutude is foundational. It is the work of the Spirit emptying the heart of self so that Christ may fill it. It is a sense of need and destitution. The meaning of "poor" in Greek means one who has nothing and is completely empty. "Poor in spirit" means that the poor are those who realize that they can never achieve salvation on their own and instead, put their complete faith and trust in Jesus Christ. It is pride, the opposite of humility that brings misery. Pride brings anger and the seeking of revenge, especially when one is offended.

How many patients are not self-assertive, self-reliant, self-confident, or self-sufficient? The poor in spirit are conscious of their sins and know in their hearts that they are completely unworthy of the grace that a most Holy God pours down upon them. The poor in spirit realize that all our assets are actually liabilities before God.

Second

"Blessed are those who mourn, for they shall be comforted."
(Matthew 5:4)

The person who mourns recognizes that he is a sinner before God. Unless convicted by the Holy Spirit that we have violated the laws of God, we may not even know to repent, much less mourn our current state of sinfulness. It is the kind of mourning that brings unbelievable joy and hope to the believer. The promise to those who mourn is that they will be comforted.

Third

"Blessed are the meek, for they shall inherit the earth."
(Matthew 5:5)

The Greek word for meek, *praus,* refers to mildness of disposition, gentleness of spirit. In this scripture, the word refers to a strong person who is under control--a God-controlled person, in thought, word, will, emotion and action. Faith is trust. The meek person trusts the Almighty as foundational, knowing that the past, present and future rest with God. Humility of soul is the primary application of the third Beatitude, the quality of spirit found in one who has been schooled to mildness by discipline and suffering and brought into resignation to the will of God. Contentment of mind is one of the fruits of meekness of spirit.

Fourth

"Blessed are they who hunger and thirst for righteousness, for they shall be satisfied." (Matthew 5:6)

Righteousness, or being in complete accordance with what is just, honorable, and Godly. Marks of a righteous person would be one who is upright, virtuous, noble, morally right and ethical. Because the indwelling Christ guides such a person's actions, one-ness of heart, conscience, soul, and spirit are visible. Here, the eye of the soul is turned away from self toward God for a very special reason: there is a longing for righteousness that I know I need. God's righteousness is synonymous with God's salvation. *Such a one whom God now calls a "saint"* (First Corinthians 1:2), is to experience an ongoing filling: not with wine, but with spirit. He will be filled with the peace of God.

Fifth

"Blessed are the merciful for they shall obtain mercy."
(Matthew 5:7)

Mercy is love toward those who are miserable, wretched and those that need some type of help or assistance. Characterized by their tender-heartedness, these people truly feel in the deepest parts of their being the pain and the suffering of those who need mercy. Most importantly, these special individuals go out of their way to make the effort to help. God shows us mercy, not when we are good but when we are miserable, helpless, wicked, ungodly and powerless. Instead of wrath, God is compassionate toward us, freely justifies us, forgives our sins, extends his mercy upon us and fills us with loving-kindness. *"He delights in mercy"* *(Micah 7:18).* Corporal (belonging to the body) words of mercy include: feeding the hungry, giving drink to the thirsty, clothing the naked, sheltering the homeless, comforting the imprisoned, visiting the sick and burying the dead. Spiritual Words of mercy include: admonishing sinners, instructing the uninformed, counseling the doubtful, comforting the sorrowful, being patient with those in error, forgiving offenses and praying each of them. If my attitude is not in check after the change-of-shift report, I count on the Holy Spirit's nudging to remind me of how fortunate I am, blessed to be a blessing!

Sixth

"Blessed are the pure of heart, for they shall see God."
(Matthew 5:8)

Evil thoughts and greed, slander and arrogance come from the hearts of men. "how can the believer keep his heart pure? By keeping it according to the Word of God." (Psalm 119:9)

"That which proceeds out of man, that is what defiles the man. For from within, out of the heart of men, proceed the evil thoughts, fornications, thefts, murders, adulteries, deed of coveting and wickedness, as well as deceit, sensuality, envy, slander, pride and foolishness. All these things proceed from within the man, and they defile the man." (Mark 7:20-23)

How can we be pure in our hearts? In our imaginations, our thoughts and our words, in our decision-making and in our desires? The truth is that we cannot do it on our own. Recognition of our impurity leads us to the path where a pure heart begins. Secondly, God must cleanse us. The pure in heart are those who are free from evil desires and evil purposes. And this is a sheer gift of grace. In Romans 8:29, God tells us that He wants *"to conform us to the image and likeness of His Son."* When we become born again and completely surrender ourselves in Jesus Christ and put our entire faith and trust in him, God will supernaturally regenerate us and give us a brand new nature. We become a new creation. Seeing God "right now" is not with eyes, but through our spiritual vision. *"God looks at the heart."* (1 Samuel 6:7) He looks upon the whole inner being, including understanding, affections and the will. This Beatitude includes both the heart received at regeneration and the transformation of character that follows God's work of grace in the soul. *First, there is "washing of regeneration" (Titus 3:5) and then "leaning of the conscience." (Hebrews 10:22)* This results in the inner realization that "being justified by faith, we have peace with God through our Lord Jesus Christ.

Seventh

"Blessed are the peacemakers, for they shall be called sons of God. (Matthew 5:11)

Peacemakers are those children of God who not only have great love for God but also have love for all of mankind and will do everything possible for the advancement of peace. Once peace is broken, they have a great desire to recover it as quickly as possible. A peacemaker is not an appeaser, but rather one who through strength and Godly knowledge endeavors to establish a right relationship between estranged parties based on truth and righteousness.

Eighth

"Blessed are those who are persecuted for righteousness'
sake, for theirs is the kingdom of heaven." (Matthew 5:12)

The persecution mentioned here is not for doing misdeeds or evil acts, but for doing righteousness. The Godly life of true believers places a distinguishing brand upon them that separates them from the rest of the world. *"The Word of God is a stumbling block to the ungodly." (1 Peter 2:8)* The unrepentant feels guilt; it becomes very easy for him to lash out at the believers of God, blaming them for making him feel bad. The world hates Jesus because He is light, righteousness and truth. He reveals the wickedness of the people of the world by exposing their evil. It is service for God that calls forth the fiercest opposition. Disciples should expect to endure 1) reviling or verbal abuse, 2) persecution, 3) harassment and 3) defamation of character. Christ's subjects are not pride-fully self-sufficient, but consciously humble. Having received mercy themselves, they are merciful in their dealings with others.

The Lord pronounced blessed, or happy those who are called upon to suffer. They are blessed because they are given privilege of having fellowship with the sufferings of the Savior, *"that I may know Him and the power of His resurrection, and the fellowship of His sufferings, being conformed to His death." (Philippians 3:10)* Such tribulation works patience and patience experiences, and experience, hope.[1]

✳ ✳ ✳

If life were only as simple as doing it Jesus' way! Repeatedly in the Bible, Jesus talks of perception. It was clear that He was needed to relate to humans in a way that no one else could relate. *"Seeing, they do not perceive..." (Matthew 13:13)* Jesus was so pure that He was not tainted with the evil that surrounded Him. He saw to the core of issues and addressed everyone and everything at the heart level.

Followers listened to Him and their whole body was transformed--mind, body, and spirit. When the disciples misjudged others, Jesus taught them. If they absolutely did not understand a concept, Jesus used parables to teach them.

Often, He would use children as examples...children because they can become the leaders of adults. They are less jaded in their thinking, more prone to listen and quite open in matters of the heart. *"on giving the paralytic a command to 'arise, take up your bed, and go to your house'" (Mark 2:8)* Jesus gave him actions to take. When He forgave him of his sins, the cripple was free to take the action and walk. It would not have happened if his sins had not been forgiven. In Mark 8:17 *"Do you still not perceive or understand?"*

When Jesus was thinking about the attitude of the Pharisees, the disciples missed the message--they were thinking of bread. They did not seem to have the eyes or ears of faith able to comprehend the true power of God and Jesus' deeds. In the Books of Acts 28:26, Jesus says, *"You will indeed look, but never perceive."* This quotation is cited five times in the New Testament to explain rejections of gospel truth. The Ten Commandments given to Moses on Mount Sinai in the Old Testament Book of Exodus, relates a series of "Thou shalt-not's," evils one must avoid in daily life on earth. In contrast, the message of Jesus was one of humility, charity and brotherly love. He taught transformation of the inner person. The first Beatitude is foundational. It is the work of the Spirit emptying the heart of self so that Christ may fill it. It is a sense of need and destitution.

Humans are unique in our ability to perceive. God gifted us with the ability to scan the environment and react uniquely, either alone or in concert with others. When I perceive "balance," I am settled in my best attitude. My physical being (material part) is cared for in its best shape, while my intuition (mind, will and emotions) completes the spiritual side. Luke tells us in Chapter Seventeen that *"the Kingdom is within."* God is Spirit and the spiritual nature is in tune with God. As I learn to listen, I define spiritual growth and more importantly, spiritual need. In the nursing realm, when I negate that internal voice, I am wrong 100% of the time. We are an incarnated soul, an integrated being, one person. Because we are spirit in a living body, we can relate to both physical and spiritual need of others.

Love is imprinted--implanted! The spiritual aspect of our being permeates all others when we are in balance. Our decisions are clear, ethics are upheld and the quality of our character is apparent since we are accountable not just to nursing, but to God. The field of nursing is not only our destiny--it is our drive. When love is practiced, the greatest law of God, the law of unconditional love is fulfilled. Patience and perseverance mark the nurse who is fulfilling his or her calling. In the Old Testament, prophets and priests existed to act as intermediaries with God; in modern times, prayer and practice of presence with patients allow God's healing touch to flow through willing vehicles. That vehicle may be a person, it may be nature, and it may be an invisible personal reassurance. Where the waters get muddied, I believe, comes as individuals overstep their areas of influence and become drawn back to our egocentric selves.

If we have incomplete perceptions, which we practically always do, our minds fill in the rest. Everywhere that Jesus went, He drew a crowd. With the title of "Rabbi" He used individual cases or parables as illustrations. We who teach are wise to consider and learn from His example.[2] Three techniques used in nursing education are: illustration, inquiry and demonstration.

1. *Illustration* - Jesus uses images from daily life--yeast, light, salt, and seed. From uneducated peasants to temple priests, early followers all had an opportunity to learn. Humility was one topic that He taught repeatedly.

2. *Inquiry* - Jesus taught through questioning, asking for more than recall or syntheses of information.
   a. Who of you by worrying can add a single hour to his life? (Matthew 6:27)
   b. What can a man be given in exchange for His soul? (Matthew 6:27)
   c. Who is my mother and who are my brothers? (Mark 8:36)

3. *Demonstration* - Jesus lived among those He taught. He walked with them, ate with them and healed in their presence. Everything Jesus did demonstrated what He came to teach: Who God is; How God loved; and How God wants us to love.

SUMMARY
CHAPTER SIX - PERCEPTION IS 100%

Nursing is unique in its grounding with one foot in the sciences and one in religion. Body-Mind-Spirit balance reveals to us the patient-centered balance that is the goal of each hospitalized person. God's order was underscored as the Almighty prepared the hearts of those who needed change. Seeking a *right heart* is crucial to progress. God's rule for helping us to mature takes many forms. In this instance, the humility of Christ and His followers is resurrected.

Blessed are the pure in spirit, for theirs is the Kingdom of Heaven.

Blessed are those who mourn, for they shall be comforted.

Blessed are the meek, for they shall inherit the earth.

Blessed are they who hunger and thirst for righteousness' sake, for they shall be satisfied.

Blessed are the merciful, for they shall obtain mercy.

Blessed are the pure in heart for they shall see God.

Blessed are the peacemakers, for they shall be called sons of God.

Blessed are those who are persecuted, for theirs is the Kingdom of Heaven.

The Lord pronounced, "blessed" those called upon to suffer. The privilege of suffering allows us to relate to our Lord and Savior

QUESTIONS
CHAPTER SIX - PERCEPTION IS 100%

1. Of the eight Beatitudes, name three that you prioritize as most important to you today. Explain why.

2. Our perception of God begins as a child. Why is it important for us to mature in the faith as we become adults?

3. Tribulation in us works patience leading to experience, and experience leading to hope. What does this progression mean to you?

RESOURCES

1. St. Gregory of Nyssa, *The Lord's Prayer and the Beatitudes, Ancient Christian Writer Series,* Mahwah: Paulist Press. http://www.jesuschristsaciro.net/Beatitudes.html

2. Jamison, Sandra (2007, *"Called to Teach: How Did Jesus Teach?",* Journal of Christian Nursing, Volume 24:1 January-March

CHAPTER SEVEN
MY EARLY YEARS

Children learn what they live. My earliest memories take me back to play at Mom's feet. She was sewing, and I was too. She taught me to make little round cloth circles for a quilt and I was actually getting proficient. I still have the very first coin purse I made at age three. She would sing and hum; we talked about everything. With the purr of the sewing machine, I felt right at home and I knew she was always there to answer my questions. Playing at her feet kind of became a ritual. We had a routine at home. Once I started grade school, the "sewing times" were moved to afternoons after school. In from school, a snack and then play until Dad got home from work. I wondered about everything. While my world and questions centered in the home at first, they eventually expanded to the school situations and topics of every kind. I probably asked "why" more than any kid I knew. Mom broke into song... "Tell me why the stars do shine...

tell me why the ivy twines..." And so my world of safety and comfort continued as I was cared for and nurtured.

I am the oldest of four children. My brother, four years younger, presented the usual sibling challenges...and joys. We played hard. When we lived in an apartment, the street outside was empty enough that my bike and his scooter could travel unobstructed. The woods behind our house afforded all kinds of opportunities...bugs to find, turtles to chase and tadpoles to follow in the pond at the bottom of the hill. I thought about the life cycle of the insects, the life cycle of the frog, and I was awed by the order of God's creation.

Our routines stood out as very comforting. We each had chores and knew that our free time depended upon their completion. The weekends were filled with swimming in the summers and ice-skating in the winter. Dad was a real athlete. He taught us from the first to appreciate sports and gave us tips on tennis and swimming. My brother and I were even on a swim team one summer. As we progressed in school, I remember helping my brother with spelling one night. The whole family got involved if one of us didn't understand something. That year the spelling of "purple" was a roadblock for him. At first I got frustrated with all the repetitions, but now looking back, it brings a smile to my memory since we all knew the whole family would help. My paternal grandmother gave us word contests when we went to her house. How many words (timed) could be made from...(she would pick a word.) Little did I know how that would prepare me for the spelling bee contest a couple years down the road.

Studies came easily for me. I completely lost myself in books and continued to ask the "why" questions, much as I had done before. I vividly remember my learning catapulting to new heights in the 4th and 5th grades. My teachers were visibly taking us to the next thinking level and I awaited each day's surprises. When my mind would drift, I had no problem filling it with imagination. I could easily listen to the teacher and be thinking about two or three other subjects simultaneously. It became a habit. I didn't even see myself drifting into the nervous energy arena.

Our church, an Evangelical Lutheran church, provided balance in our week. We were involved individually and as a family. I sang in the youth choir and chaired the youth fellowship when I became old enough. The UNICEF (United Nations Infants and Children's Emergency Fund) campaign highlighted fall activities and our annual paper drive introduced us to the neighbors in our area. Life was full and life was fun. I loved to cook; it was my job to make the cookies for the vacation. In fact, I would get so excited, I would become physically sick the night before we were due to leave home. Fortunately, I grew out of that one. My family of origin expanded when Mom re-married and gave birth to my sisters, born one year apart. This provided a great training ground for my teenage baby-sitting years. I remember bouncing them on my knee as toddlers and planning my life with a houseful of these bundles of energy. You can't kiss babies enough!

I pondered the cycle of life as I saw the joy of my toddler sisters and thought about the emotional development of children at each stage of physical development. Initially, a baby is not ready to do more than drink milk and respond to Mama. The toddler matures and is fascinated by the environment around her. God's handiwork is very ordered. As we are nurtured and come to realize that we are each unique, He waits for our caretakers to instill the secrets of abiding life; abiding in Him is the key.

I began my search to discover the stages of faith development in the child.

Several paradigms described in literature identify developmental faith stages across the life span. Psychologist James Fowler proposed one of the first and most frequently cited trajectories of faith development for most children.[1] These stages include:

1. *Undifferentiated faith* - essentially a pre-stage, exists when an infant's trust is developed through parental bonding.
2. *Intuitive-projective faith* - approximately 3-6 years (pre-school to early primary school age) when the child has much fantasy and learns by parental stories and examples.
3. *Mythic-literal faith* - around 7-12 years (elementary school age) during which a child begins to identify with his or her own faith or religious tradition.
4. *Synthetic-conventional faith* - (adolescent years from 13-20) when the teen compares his or her own faith with other belief systems such as those of peers.

There is a poem that reminds me of the delicate nature of a child's psyche by Dorothy Nolte called, "Children Learn What They Live." On days when child care tested my limits, I would read this poem to remind myself how important my words and actions were. In the poem Nolte writes that if children live with criticism, hostility, ridicule and shame, they learn to condemn, fight, be shy and feel guilty. If, on the other hand, they live with tolerance, encouragement, praise, fairness, security and approval, they learn to be patient, confident, appreciative and just. In short, they learn to have faith and to like themselves. Acceptance and friendship gird them for the challenges ahead. The poem always reminds me of the power of our words —especially to children. Criticism leads to condemnation, hostility leads to fighting, ridicule to shyness and shame to guilt, whereas the values of positive reinforcement produce patience, confidence, appreciation, justice, faith, self-love and a search for love in the world.

In the Book of Deuteronomy, basic family values are addressed. The home is the natural place for values to be taught. This can only happen as positive choices are presented and rewarded. Infants and young children develop social and emotional skills that progress sequentially.[2] A child learns initially from the trust developed with Mom and caregivers as ties expand to the family members where he or she lives. Beyond the boundaries of the home, society becomes the testing ground for what lies ahead. Rights and responsibilities are taught from the time the child is old enough to reason and follow directions. Safety measures taught in the home include the dangers of hot stoves, unsecured stairs, heaters, boiling water, knives, etc. in preparation for the outside world.

How will he or she learn to make choices? Only by allowing the child choices will they be prepared for success. These choices may be as simple as what to eat, what to wear and appropriate manners in public. It is the process of choosing that is important. The practice of praise is paramount. A good rule of thumb is "Praise in public; discipline in private." Consequences of the child's choices must be honored. It is important to stay away from emotional responses such as anger or hostility. A child learns to define and take ownership of his or her actions when natural consequences follow. Warmth, acceptance and consistency were all important in our household.

Key concepts in communicating with children center on positive words. For example, "I like it when you..." or "It is helpful when you clean your room." Every step we take models behavior to a child, from the first moment their eyes rest on us in the morning until they are tucked into bed at night. If Mom or Dad is upset, the child will automatically assume it is because of him or her. If we are overbearing or angered, the child may respond in kind. At the same time, a child's behavior has to be corrected when it is wrong. "We are discussing your behavior," is a way to communicate this.

Allowing the child to make choices teaches the child the better avenue to take. When things go awry, there is no "one size fits all." Discipline helps the child develop conscience, the internalized voice that will guide him in making decisions for the rest of his/her life.

My childhood memories of church and learning about God's love spanned nature and people. I learned that Jesus was God's Son and he was love. As a child of God, I was very special to Our Creator too. Respect, honor and obedience marked lessons about doing God's will, and I wanted to please my family and God with my choices and service. Most importantly, I learned that life happens step by step. I was never scolded for something that I didn't know about or in those situations where I had not participated. Consistency was a given in our household and knowing the boundaries made life easier.

Three parental types name by the Child Development Association - *authoritative, authoritarian and permissive.* I fortunately experienced the authoritarian. Children of *authoritative* parents (I am in charge; you will do it my way) are timid, rebellious, fearful and hungry for attention. Children of *authoritarian* parents (there are rules, but parent is not demanding) have standards, but these are given with love. The child is treated as a human being and is open to questioning and learning. He/she is positive and self-assured. *Permissive* parents parent children who do not respond to authority. They are open to danger and become risk takers without restraint. Balance of body, mind and spirit is begun with a balance of work and play during childhood.

Emotional health rests with experiences that reinforce selected behaviors and recognition of warning signs that signal danger. Understanding *love as Jesus loved* paints a picture of total understanding for me. Jesus related to children throughout his teachings, often using them as examples of those who are open to new ideas and truth. There is a place in God's heart that each of us can fill. We are not born with dysfunctional love. Dysfunctional love is learned, just as every memory is indelibly printed on a child's mind. "The nature of everything involved in the life of God in us is only discerned when we have been through it and it is in our past."[3] With each new learned experience, the child establishes new associations, new bonds, new connections. A child is taught by active as well as passive influences.

Children learn of God visually in the garden, in the stars and moon in the night sky, and by the birds singing in the morning. God sends messages, even through our adult lives through people that surround us. The most important thought or communication that we learn is the language of love. God designed it that way, taught us what it means to love, and sent our role model, His precious Son, Jesus Christ.

SUMMARY
CHAPTER SEVEN - MY EARLY YEARS

Basic family values are taught in the Book of Deuteronomy. Home is the proper place for role modeling, for questions to be answered and for positive choices to be rewarded. Infants and children develop social and emotional skills that progress sequentially. A child learns from the initial trust developed with Mom and caregivers to the family in which they operate. Rights and responsibilities are taught from the time the child is old enough to reason and follow directions.

What skills will the child need for functioning in the outside world? How will the child learn to make choices? Only with choices can a child develop the habit of being successful by any measure. It is the process of choosing that is important.

The practice of praise is paramount. It is critically important to remember to "praise" in public" and "discipline in private." By reinforcing the positive, i.e., "I like it when you..."" The child learns to be comfortable with loving correction and re-directing of his or her efforts. Regardless of the state of the relationship, the child has you in focus from the time his or her eyes rest on you in the morning until he or she slides into bed at night. If Mom and Dad are receptive and open to what is happening around them, it is good to have an agreed upon timeline. Likewise, if Mom or Dad is upset, the child will automatically feel that it is because of him or her.

Balance of body, mind and spirit is begun with the balance of work and play as a child. Emotional health rests with experiences that reinforce selected behaviors. Jesus often used children to teach lessons to the disciples and their followers. A child's mind is open, open and receptive. With each new learned experience, the child establishes new associations, new bonds and new connections. The most important thought or communications that your child can learn is the language of love. God designed it that way, taught us what it means by covenanting with us. The greatest of all gifts was the present, His precious Son. There is a place in our heart that only God can fill.

QUESTIONS
CHAPTER SEVEN - MY EARLY YEARS

1. Consistency and praise are critically important in dealing with children. Please explain why.

2. Psychologist James Fowler identifies developmental faith stages across the life span. List each of the four types and differentiate between them.

3. Our words and actions are seen, heard and lived out by our children. What actions taken by your parents/guardians rest in your memory, positive or negative?

4. Basic family values are taught in the Book of Deuteronomy. Why are positive choices so important in the child's development?

5. Discipline helps the child develop conscience. (T/F) Explain how.

6. The child Development Association describes three parental "types" - authoritative, authoritarian, and permissive. Explain the differences and rank the three types from "least desired" to "most desired."

RESOURCES

1. Fowler, James, (1981), S*tages of Faith: the Psychology of Human Development and the Quest for Meaning,* San Francisco: Harper Publishers. Page 162

2. State of Connecticut (1998), *Birth to Three System Service Guidelines,* December. Page 9

3. Chambers, Oswald (1995), *My Utmost for His Highest Devotional Journal,* Grand Rapids: Discovery House Publishers, Page April 30th

CHAPTER EIGHT
GROWTH THROUGH SCARS

The telephone rang and my Mom answered. Saturday morning was my weekly time to check in on her in Baltimore, Maryland, my hometown. This particular day, I was completely spent. I had worked hard all week, and on top of that drained my memory of past events during counseling; events that I had managed for years to avoid telling my mother. As she answered the telephone, Mom's voice was too magnetic. In her soft intuitive way, she said "Donna, there's something wrong, what is it?" I was silent at first and then told her a secret that had tormented me since childhood.

"Mom, I was raped when I was sixteen." As the words came out, I wanted to take them back, to withhold the piercing reality that I knew would crush her. I immediately dissolved into tears, and through the sobbing, told her the whole truth that I had buried for thirty-five years.

Mom was always in tune with each of us. We shared happy times and sad times; she was always there to cheer us on or offer a shoulder for us to cry on. There had never been a stronger bond than that of my Mom and me. We shared every avenue of life. I put myself in her place and tried to assuage the tremendous sadness and regret that I knew she felt.

Little was I prepared for the wrath that would follow, not from Mom but from the rest of my family for upsetting her. When I explained the trauma (rape) to my sisters, they didn't understand why I had not confided it to them. I am sure in the same situation, I would have felt left out. My reply was, "You were 10 years younger at the time. It wouldn't have been appropriate." I prayed for understanding-both by my relatives and also for me.

It is difficult enough to address conflict issues in person; it is quite another to try to solve problems long distance. Our family's relationship with the perpetrator's family had long been split, releasing me from any obligation to make a visit home which would clearly have created severe and painful repercussions. Only with God at my side was I able to get through the following days. By this time in my recovery and healing, I knew that I was well on my way to forgiving the harm done to me. I also knew God was with me and, with God's help, I could handle the barrage of telephone calls from family members, though the rift which began that day has yet to be reconciled.

For years, I wrongfully thought that by burying the assault, even the memory would eventually go away. This was not true, I also needed God's protection in dealing with the outcome scenarios during the subsequent years. I was now able to move forward with healing, leaving behind the past and its mental chains.

Even in the midst of such a negative chain of events, there were positives that were so strong. What had God blessed me with that I could take from the experience? How would I be asked to use it, if at all? What insights could help to prevent a similar attack in the future? I prayed for guidance. I prayed for emotional healing. Strengthened by God I had absolute faith that I would be restored.

Mom and Dad had given a solid foundation of family values and the steps to find solutions even with situations as painful and complex as this. We learned independence by stretching out beyond the family and in turn by helping others. Loving, caring responses to our good deeds as well as our foibles laid a solid groundwork for our walks through life. I prayed and I prayed hard. I wanted so much to make the situation better; in reality, I finally had to accept that I could only be responsible for my own feelings and my own actions.

Like love, family ties and friendships are harder to strengthen and maintain long distance. I spent years feeling guilty about not visiting home more often. My husband's work schedule, absence and my job in the military created too many obstacles. Over the months and years that followed, I projected what I would say to Mom to get other issues from the past out in the open. But the hurt I so often saw in her eyes kept me from speaking up. In Mom's young life, I witnessed a woman who had gone through a stormy marriage and divorce, then cared for her own mother during a terminal illness, and after giving birth to a son with polio, was widowed at the age of twenty-one. Despite her amazing strength and the knowledge that she would protect us at all cost, Mom was the gentlest human being I had ever known.

In retrospect, I should have trusted in the tremendous love and support that she always gave. The secret I kept for all those years actually removed the choice from her to respond to the situation, but the pain was too intense and made me reluctant to inflict any more pain on her. I now realized that the reason I felt like "running" when under stress was directly related to the incident. Many, many past behaviors were beginning to make sense. Whenever I perceived being "held down" or "held back," I immediately reacted with the "flight" escape mechanism.

In researching bio-behavioral responses to stress, Freeman and company delineate two powerful tools. The fight or flight response represents a genetically hard-wired early warning system designed to alert us to external environmental threat posing a danger to our physical survival. Because survival is the supreme goal, the system is highly sensitive, set to register extremely minute levels of potential danger. The fight or flight response not only warns us of real external danger but also of the mere perception of danger. A safe environment is critical. Physical safety means getting out of hostile environments; emotional safety means surrounding ourselves with friends and people who genuinely care for us. Spiritual safety means creating a life surrounded with a sense of purpose including a relationship with a higher power and a resolve to release deeply held feelings of shame, worthlessness and excessive guilt.

Emotions are the center of aptitudes for living.[1] "They prepare the body physiologically for a different response. With *anger*, the blood flows to the hands making it easier to grasp a weapon or strike a foe; heart-rate increases and a rush of hormones generates a pulse of energy. With *fear*, blood flows to the large skeletal muscles such as legs, making it easier to flee. The emotion of *happiness* inhibits negative feelings with available energy quieting worry. The relaxation response, or *love*, generates a state of calm and contentment, facilitating cooperation. Eyes widen during the *surprise* response to evaluate the option and make a plan. In *disgust,* the upper lip curls to one side. *Sadness* brings a drop in energy and enthusiasm; metabolism slows.[2]

The messages from our society had influenced me to bury my problems and deny their existence. I chose to believe that I needed only to do a job in order to progress and be promoted, loved and cared for. I couldn't have been more wrong! I wasn't aware at the time, of the cost to me in spiritual pain. The years I spent suppressing it were futile because at different times in my career certain events and situations triggered memories of the rape. At times, the staff or my patients would say something that triggered a visceral response in my gut, but I would just ignore the clues that I was out of balance. I gradually spun out of control, with my life going deeper in turmoil. Objective remarks from well-meaning colleagues were perceived by me as attacks. Because I personalized such observations, I was sometimes unable to receive constructive feedback. This tendency caused me to be misunderstood even when I had compassion or understanding that was far deeper than the surface emotions the patients or staff relayed. I could tell by the face of others that there was a barrier of misjudgment hindering my effectiveness.

My escalating stress behaviors peeled away my ego defenses until I felt totally stripped of my identity. At this point, the relationships with Mom and with God helped me to begin healing. Both signified love and both provided all the peace that I needed. During a two-year period, many opportunities for healing came to me. The first coincided with the first six months of counseling. I was offered the opportunity to teach Spiritual Gifts at our church. Through those classes I came to realize just how many God-given gifts I had been granted; and, it was painful to see that others did not see their giftedness.

The next project that aided my healing was even larger. It involved special training in the area of "Prevention of Domestic Violence." I traveled to Austin, Texas for the State of Texas training as a counselor. The tears streamed down my face. I recognized myself in the behaviors that were described and I saw my family's scenario played over and over again. I remember feeling that I had done something wrong every time there was an argument at home. I felt loved but didn't want Mom to be yelled at because of me - ever. I was confused. I knew how to make her happy and that was always my goal. I never saw love personified more than with my precious Mom. There was no doubt in my mind that my intuition, patient sensitivity and insight began right there in Mom's presence.

At the conference, I watched the videos, internalized the slides, and saw familiar scenes of patients with whom I'd chaperoned in the emergency room or the gynecology clinic. Statistics were displayed of shocking results - of the number of females who experience the violence of rape. One in three was the statistic at that time and programs were mushrooming that offered resources for care, shelter and education. Experienced in counseling, I found upon my return home that I was able to counsel individuals from my church.

My husband and I opened a Spouse Abuse Shelter while we were stationed overseas in Japan. The pastors called us to respond to a telephone call for help in the neighborhood. As awareness of this community problem grew in our congregation, the need for education became readily apparent. A program was instituted to educate the staff member and volunteers. Telephone triage of necessary questions was streamlined and added to the orientation. Working with the staff of the church, a dedicated effort was put in place to educate the congregation, offer safety tips and afford women the opportunity to call "safe" contact telephone numbers for counseling or crisis intervention. A Statement of Belief regarding Prevention of Domestic Violence was developed and implemented at our church. It is now part of the church staff orientation.

Recognition of the patterns of domestic violence is the first step in seeking help. Because domestic violence or abuse occurs in intimate relationships, it may take the form of coercion, threats, intimidation, isolation and emotional, sexual and physical abuse.[3] "Batterers" do tend to take their anger out on their intimate partner. Key to the person seeking help is the realization that an abusive relationship is about power and control. The abuser aims to instill fear and wanting to have power and control in the relationship. But it's not really about anger.[4]

In an abusive relationship, the abuser may use varying tactics to gain power and control including: 1) Children as pawns - accuses you of bad parenting, threatens to take the children away, uses the children to relay messages or threatens to report you to children's protective services. 2) Coercion and threats - threatens to hurt other family members, pets, children or self, 3) Denial and blame - Denies that the abuse occurs and shifts responsibility for the abusive behavior onto you, 4) Economic abuse - controls finances, refuses to share money, makes you account for money spent and doesn't want you to work outside the home, 5) Emotional abuse - uses put-downs, insults, criticism or name-calling to make you feel bad about yourself, 6) Intimidation - uses certain looks, actions or gestures to instill fear - the abuser may break things, destroy property, abuse pets or display weapons, 7) Isolation - limits your contact with family and friends, requires you to get permission to leave the house, doesn't allow you to work or attend school, and controls your activities and social events. The abuser may ask where you've been, track your time and whereabouts, or check the odometer on your car, 8) Power - makes all major decisions, defines the roles in your relationship, is in charge of the home and social life, and treats you like a servant or possession. "It's important to know that these relationships don't happen overnight," reports Patterson. "It's a gradual process-a slow disintegration of a person's sense of self."

✱ ✱ ✱

Hindsight is always 20/20. I know now that the healing path for me involved specific choices. As the underlying problem surfaced, I first and foremost prayed that God would provide the right steps and people. I found the right Christian Counselor, the right medical physician (to rule out medical issues) and the right spiritual director to shepherd me through the days ahead. He will also provide you yours.

DOMESTIC VIOLENCE POLICY

August, 1999

Presented by the Health Ministry's Domestic Violence Task Force at our San Antonio Methodist Church

1. We will not tolerate abuse in the family, work place, or society.

2. We affirm the United Methodist statement on Family Violence and Abuse (Discipline, 1996, paragraph 65H); "We recognize that family violence and abuse in all its forms--- verbal, psychological, physical, economic, sexual is detrimental to the covenant of human community. We encourage the church to provide a safe environment, counsel, and support for the victim. While we deplore the actions of the abuser, we affirm that person to be in need of God's redeeming love."

3. We will include anti-abuse information in pre-marital, marital, and individual counseling. Information about Domestic Violence awareness will be presented in appropriate programs for all age groups, and be available through brochure and card form.

SUMMARY
CHAPTER EIGHT - GROWTH THROUGH SCARS

There is no greater love than God's love. Introduced to us through our natural mothers, we learn physical, emotional and spiritual connectedness. The foundational bonds formed in my family of origin were strengthened with each new test of life. Only with God at my side was I able to handle the trauma caused by a rape. The fact that this person was a trusted family member made the recovery even more difficult.

For self-preservation and with the coping capabilities of a teenager, I took the easiest route I knew and buried the incident. Thinking that the pain and complexity of relationships would dissipate through the years, I didn't realize how I had been set up for a jaded view of men and their intentions. I guarded myself carefully as best I could, shying away from anything that signaled danger to me in relationships or circumstances. I often viewed objective feedback of co-workers or supervisors as an attack. This tendency caused me to be misunderstood, even when I had compassion or understanding far deeper than the surface emotions relayed by patients or staff.

God proceeded to turn my hurt into a blessing. After intensive counseling and a reliving of the horrors of that night, I grew to learn that no longer did this have a hold on my being. I was free, finally of all the barriers that in the past thwarted my future-view. Prevention of domestic violence became the focus of a wellness program at our church and was a perfect introduction to help the hurting in my immediate circle of influence.

I began to appreciate the height, depth, breadth and width of God's love. I loved through the tragedy into forgiveness; I loved beyond hate, beyond burden, beyond human negativity. I truly saw the heart of another. it was then and only then that I could thank God for the thorns.

QUESTIONS
CHAPTER EIGHT - GROWTH THROUGH SCARS

1. Describe the fight, flight or freeze mechanism when trauma is introduced.

2. What role do familial relationships play in a scenario involving an assault against a family member?

3. Prevention of Domestic Violence became a focus for our church. How does specialized training (Domestic Violence) assist the professional to cope with traumas?

4. Define the dimensions of love that you recognize in this story. In your story?

RESOURCES

1. Goleman, Daniel (1995), New York: Bantam Books, *Emotional Intelligence*, Page xiii.

2. Ibid, Page xiv

3. Mayo Clinic, *"Domestic Violence Toward Women: recognize the Patterns and Seek help,"* 2005. Rochester: http://www.mayoclinic.com/healthy/domestic-violence WO00044

4. Patterson, Diane, Mayo Clinic

CHAPTER NINE
SURRENDER AND PROMISE

Does surrender to God insulate us from disloyalty, pain betrayal or the misuse of power? I don't believe it does, and one incident caught me completely off guard but resourced me with a variety of lessons on *worldly power*. Soon after my total submission to God, I experienced an event that has had a profound effect every time I re-live it. For those of us who were interested, the church offered an opportunity to develop an outreach group designed to support families of the incarcerated. "*I was in prison and you visited me.*" (Matthew 25:36) My reaction to the prison visit was so profound as a means of grace, I was elated to be involved in a new way for the families of those in prison. After all, I had just witnessed administrative power and the damage that wrong-doing can bring. Maybe I could help the inmates' families.

As a fledgling group, the by-laws stated that an advisory council be formed to include the lay directors, spiritual directors and prison representatives in preparation for a spiritual retreat weekend called a "walk." In the second year of the group's existence, I was scheduled to be the Lay Director, or Coordinator for the walk, to make administrative decisions about the flow of events and insure that the rules were followed.

When I received a telephone call from a member of the advisory council requesting my presence at a meeting the next evening, I asked who would be there, and was told "a national representative, to review some things." Sensing trouble, I then asked my husband if he would attend the meeting with me. Upon entering the room, I found a huge round table of approximately thirteen people, none of whom I recognized. My intuition was proven right--there sat my judges, but I felt safe...my husband was on my right and my spiritual director for the walk was on my left! I have looked at the faces of naysayers before and I recognized their stares immediately. My positive perspective was more than they wanted—and I was to be squelched before the walk began.

The complaint was that my predecessor (the previous Lay Director) did not agree with my handling of the team and wanted to make it very clear that her way of operation was the only way. The more we discussed matters, the farther the group moved in opposition to me. Every response from their leader was, "Yes, those are the words (in the manual), but that's not what they mean." Logic clearly eluded my accusers and didn't help me at all. Their agenda was to block any pattern of creativity that I saw as helpful and stop the process before the walk ever came to fruition. I counted on God's wisdom to guide me and had surrendered the outcome of that meeting to My Lord before I entered the room. Explanations to non-receptive, agenda-filled receivers might as well be mute. As it turned out,

I was asked to continue the duties as lay director. Is the memory still painful? Yes. But I learned that ultimately, it's not my battle and if I am going to allow God to use me for higher purposes, I must receive the ability to surrender all my power to God's control. The anatomy and dynamic interaction of the team was a powerful witness during that fall weekend; lifetime changes were made in the hearts of hurting pilgrims. What a blessing to be able to see the difference!

"Do you have eyes and fail to see? Do you have ears and fail to hear? Then Jesus laid his hands on his eyes again; and he looked intently and his sight was restored, and he saw everything clearly." (Mark 8:18, 25)

The key to body-mind-spirit balance is our understanding of God. Trust is foundational; it is with trust that we will be given courage to surrender *our* will to God's greater will. This level of trust grows with practice giving us a great measure of hope in our private and public lives. In my career, I trusted that my preparation as a nurse would be sufficient to answer the patient's questions, listen to their stated dilemmas, and protect them against the challenges that a hospitalization might bring. My trust in God made me an instrument of hope to them.

In Sister O'Brien's book, *The Nurse With An Alabaster Jar*[1], a campus minister speaks about his hospitalization and the power that the scriptural theme of hope afforded him. It is important for patients to know that God cares for them. The visits gave the minister a renewed sense of hope. Trust and hope are interchangeable.

"For God alone my soul waits in silence; for my hope is from Him." (Psalm 62:5); "You are my hiding place and my shield; I hope in your word." (Psalm 119:114);

I rise before dawn and cry for help; I put my hope in your
words." (Psalm 119:147);

"God's Chosen Servant will not break a bruised reed...and
in his name the Gentiles will hope." (Matthew 12:19, 21)

The molding of my heart has not always been easy. Some life experiences have resulted in positive outcomes, but there were also life-altering events that, at times, have frozen my heart to change. Returning to surrender and trust in God was the only way for me to continue then, and it still is now. It always takes humbly admitting to God that I cannot exist independently and still accomplish what He has prepared me to do. I surrendered control and sought daily to continue releasing any hold that I had on my being. I learned to relinquish negative feelings that I had with any and all co-workers. I repeatedly abandoned my pride and in doing so, realized the comfort and protection that came each time I was able to surrender it all to God.

In Patrick Carnes' book, *The Betrayal Bond: Breaking Free of Exploitive Relationships*[2], I found explanations of behaviors in my adult life that had taken root in my childhood. For years I didn't understand the complexity of relationships. "Betrayal intensifies pathologically the human trait of bonding deeply in the presence of danger or fear. It is a breach of trust that becomes apparent when those things that you thought to be true, were proven otherwise." According to Carnes, betrayal is a form of abandonment. When this moves into the realm of trauma, it is fear and terror that cause extraordinary changes in the neurological system and internal organs.

It is true that the mind of a child copes with what it can and represses those thoughts, words and scenes that cannot be handled at the time. I vividly remember watching a television show that replayed a scene too close to home. When the argument escalated to a certain point, a gun was pulled and aimed at the mother. I froze in my shoes. This was a scene replayed from my early childhood. As I remember it, Mom and Dad were arguing about something. I was ten years old at the time and my brother and I were just getting used to having another person in the household. I tiptoed downstairs to see what the problem was. As I rounded the corner of the hallway and passed by the open door of the master bedroom, I saw Mom at a distance, cornered, with Dad shouting, "If you don't tell me what I want to know I'll have to use this"--pulling the gun from the dresser drawer. Had I caused the argument? Was it my fault? I retreated, ran upstairs and cowered while I wondered if it was something I had done or said. Why would this man that said he loved us be threatening my only security blanket to that point, my Mom. Fear took center stage. Shock and disbelief, fear and loneliness repeated themselves with every incident, yet I was unaware of my feelings because my guard was up. Reality vs. feared reality—where was I in this scenario? Carnes states: People who live in exploitive systems do not necessarily know when they are being deceived.[3]

Stress becomes traumatic when danger, risk, fear or anxiety are present. Eight ways that trauma affects people over time include: trauma reaction, trauma arousal, trauma blocking, trauma splitting, trauma abstinence, trauma shame, trauma repetition and trauma bonds.[3] Of these, the three that I related to immediately were trauma reaction, trauma blocking (an effort to numb, block out or repress residual feelings) and trauma bonds. Efforts to block include: excessive drinking, use of depressant drugs, compulsive exercise, compulsive working and compulsive eating. Trauma bonds include the following characteristics:

1) they are seldom alone, 2) trauma bonds and their allies can form a life pattern, 3) trauma bonds can be very durable and 4) trauma bonds can happen to anyone.[4]

Five realities about trauma bonds:

1. Victims tend to recreate the trauma in some form for themselves or for others. Others recreate the trauma by identifying with the aggressor and perpetrator in the same act that was once exercised on them.
2. Betrayal by seduction - those from dysfunctional families where there is abuse are particularly vulnerable to seduction. The boundaries that prevent most people from being deceived are not there.
3. Trauma survivors can be extremely naïve, even while being vigilant. Living with secrets, denial, deception and exploitation leads to impaired discernment and common sense.
4. Trauma bonds can happen to anyone.
5. Trauma bonds are not always bad but they are about survival.[5]

Neurobiological changes occur in the body during intense fear, resulting in reactivity. The parts of the brain designed to protect the self gain dominance and may override other parts of the brain that limit reaction responses.[6] Trauma bonds for children appear to be more severe. They are experiencing their primary attachment. If terror is created in those relationships, the mind creates deep patterns and scripts. After witnessing the gun pulled on my mother, I was extremely wary of doing anything to upset Dad. Even an inkling of a wrong behavior threw me into the fight—flight or freeze mental state. I feared for myself but I feared more for Mom. She was the most important figure in my life and I knew I would do anything I could to make her life easier. The incident was never spoken of again...until thirty years later when my counselor uncovered the truth.

Even my prayers up to that point were filled with hurt, filled with un-forgiveness and marked with times of terror. As strange as it seems, when I was in a life-threatening situation, I never questioned God's presence. I did what I had to do to survive and thanked God that I was saved to live another day. As I have let go of more and more personal control and surrendered my destiny to God, there has been more and more recognition of divine protection and strength to face challenges.

Positive change requires transformation within. At times. I recognize a change in myself and at other times, I am totally blind to it. Thankfully, people have been placed around me who posses discernment and the strengths that I lack. It is beautiful to experience God's plan for us to live in community and help each other toward the greater goal of unconditional love and service. If anyone had asked me what my passion was during my military career, the answer was easy - helping people! There is no greater joy for me than to teach, nurture and counsel patients and fellow nurses. Attuned to their needs, I found myself able to respond with Godly wisdom in seeking to direct novice nurses. Their lack of experience placed barriers in the way until they realized that *caring* is more about presence; about the "being" and not always "doing" of nurse tasks.

God taught me that identity rests not with man-made rules but with *Who* and *Whose,* I am. I am able to share with others how faith absolutely overrides anything man can impose upon me and I have learned that the order that structures our society and world are simply man-made attempts to understand God's direction for us. I understood how God had protected me.

Perseverance is needed to face challenges, whether overt or more subtle. During trials, our identity in God will arm us with compassion and kindness, humility, gentleness and patience. Clothed in God's love, others may be drawn to us, but when I operate in my own power, the result is limited. On my own, I veer from my true and satisfying purposes. But when I let go and let God guide me, I am filled with peace when the right decisions are made. Sometimes, God calms the storm within me and at other times, the storms that surround me. When I live yielded to God's plan, others can see that there might be a better way than our struggle to be self-sufficient.

When I surrender and submit to Godly teachings, I receive God's promised protection and restoration and the blessed "rest" that God offers me. In retrospect, some Christian teachings purported to be soul enhancing have fallen far short of renewing guidance. I believe that there is a human tendency toward legalism that usually creeps in. From my perspective, God intends healing and wholeness for each of us. Openness to divine and unconditional love allows God's justice and mercy to take care of any problem I might encounter. Do I rest in God's care? You bet, for it is during those moments that I yield to God in complete trust! For I am assured that my abandonment to the Lord has allowed me to rest in His total care. True faith has taught me that I was never abandoned by the Lord.

SUMMARY
CHAPTER NINE - SURRENDER AND PROMISE

Because God is only good, I know that I can trust in the Creator's choice of lessons, solutions and my personal plan with each challenge presented. Surrender is comprised of *trust, transformation* and resultant *growth*. Trust involves personal confidence in God; trust in choice, not chance and above all, trust in love. God's transformation of us involves *change* and *growth* along a continuum. Obedience on our part must spring from love. I know God only sees the good in me and I can trust that the Almighty has a specifically planned program of realization for me to learn. Outside of myself, the evidence will appear to others as a difference in my approach.

The strength of my faith carried me through past challenges and I trusted that the Lord would be at my side in the days to come as well. Godly growth comes with spirit, mind and body balance. An example of this was a pastor who was hospitalized. The natural tension that comes with any of us experiencing hospitalization rang true for this pastor. When we are surrounded by the physical facility, the staff and the limitations of our own experience, we are vulnerable. The pastor found that out and relied on the Scriptures for *hope*.

The molding of my heart has not always been easy. Returning to surrender and trust in God was the only way for me to continue then, just as it is now. I surrendered control and any hold that I had on my being. God's love, justice and mercy guided me to a place of wholeness. Only with God will the promises I believed come true.

QUESTIONS
CHAPTER NINE - SURRENDER AND PROMISE

1. Surrender of my will includes what three stages?

2. I have a choice between Godly growth and my own plan. Explain how God's plan of body, mind and spirit balance far exceeds any plan I may design.

3. Regardless of my recognition of "temptations" of the old self, I must turn to God for the best positive approach. How will I know it is not my "old self" tempting me?

4. God's love, justice and mercy are evident in all that I witness here on earth. How does God's justice far exceed any "payback" that I might envision?

Chapter Nine Surrender and Promise*

RESOURCES

1. O'Brien, Mary Elizabeth (2006), The Nurse With An Alabaster Jar, Madison: Nurse Christian Fellowship Press. Page 130

2. Carnes, Patrick (1960), The Betrayal Bond, breaking Free of Exploitive Relationships, Deerfield Beach, Florida: Health Communications. Page 53

3. Ibid, Page 54

4. Ibid, Page 59

5. Ibid, Page 53.

6. Ibid, Pages 22-23

CHAPTER TEN
MOLDED FOR GOOD

I liken my metamorphosis to the process of pottery making. For the clay to be molded, it first must be worked. Not only does the heat of the potter's hand affect the clay, there must be immense pressure to form the desired object. Heat: pressure: molding –I felt it all. But God's greater plan required it! The repetitive nature of the wheel of life turning round and round brought me back to the same lessons, the same fractured place, that God needed to heal. I hadn't yet put the pieces together, but in the Master Potter's hand, I was finally ready to succumb. *"...as the clay is in the potter's hand, so are you in my hand." Jer 18:6.* Involved in three car accidents in a fifteen-month period of time during 1996 and 1997 made me realize I was overstressed. In each circumstance, I was rushing to get somewhere, rushing toward another activity or reaching for the mobile telephone, letting myself be distracted from concentrating on driving. In the third incident, my husband's car was totaled. As I reached for the phone, my eyes left the concentration of the impending traffic.

The peak of my distress, however, came in 1998 when a five-month series of events forced my hand; I had reached my limit! My best friend's twenty-two-year-old daughter collapsed and died at college, followed two months later by her husband's death due to cancer. My heart ached for my friend.

Physically, I was still jarred from the accident and continuing with physical therapy. Then I was called into my supervisor's office on a Friday morning and told that I had until 5 PM to resign. In shock, I asked on what grounds she was doing this and she showed me a statement signed when I was hired...*with or without cause prior to six months.*

Stunned, I said, "So let me get this straight; You hired me specifically to implement a program; I not only projected future needs but justified full-time positions for the staff, and now you don't need me anymore." There was silence.

Still reeling from this situation, yet another major and unexpected development caught me by surprise in that same five-month period. I was relaxing and enjoying a gathering at a friend's house for a holiday weekend dessert social. Yes, I knew everyone in the room so I relaxed immediately. As some of the guests were finishing the preparations, I took a seat in the middle of the sofa between my husband and the senior pastor. Our senior pastor took my arm under his and began to talk, "Donna, we are all very concerned about you. We want you to know how much you mean to us and we want to help." Immediately I turned to my husband for reassurance, to find that he was turned away with his arms folded so he couldn't see my face.

The pastor then began to recite the 23rd Psalm. His hold was so tight on my arm that I couldn't move; flight would have been a welcome relief at this point but the fear held me frozen. Then my circle of friends gathered around me and I knew that things would be okay; possibly, I could trust them more than myself.

During the course of the next hour, observations were shared about the increasing stress that seemed to be taking its toll on me. At that point, I wondered whether I would be admitted to the hospital and envisioned my nursing license sprouting wings and flying out of the window. But as the hour progressed, facts and feelings were shared, ending with a plan for medical evaluation, already scheduled for the next day. Through the tears, I held on to the fact that "Things could be worse; I could be admitted to the hospital right now. And whom could I trust? Weren't these the very people that made a covenant vow to take care of me?" And so they did. I had just been a part of an often-neglected witness to God's power--an intervention. Later, I was diagnosed at the Counselor's office with clinical depression.

Trusting God to make my way clear, I remained flexible to change, especially my own.

Blessed with a completely positive attitude (thank you, Mom) I held on to the fact that all of these Godly people cared enough to gather here for me. The whole crew was here - physician, pastors and friends. If the body, mind and spirit could not be helped with all this, where was the hope of getting well? My vulnerability to the whole situation made me realize how alone I felt. As I re-lived the intervention, I was angry that it involved so many people. Wasn't I the victim? Wasn't I the hurting one? In reality, it was the balance of God's love through His chosen ones that brought the relief. Each person in that room had been a part of my life. Each person cared for me and loved me enough to take the time to show me the way. I couldn't do it on my own. I was helpless.

As you can imagine, the ride home was rather silent that night, but the reality of a plan for my road to health was the goal I needed most. I glanced over to my husband after he gently broke the silence and I thought, "Here was compassion personified. I must really have scared him when my stress behaviors took over the home front." I forgave him for springing the intervention on me. In reality, that's what an intervention is all about. It's about love and the height and the depth and the breadth of God's love--shown through those who love us. "True forgiveness is to see through the eyes of Mercy to the real man created in and as the likeness of God, to cease seeing the offense of the man and to send it away from him. We separate the offense from the offender and we send the offense away...by not imputing the offense to him by not attributing it to his account."[2]

You might ask what happened. Well, the appointment and all the physical findings were normal. If there is one thing you can trust, it is a known friend that just happens to be a brilliant physician as well. The Medical Resonance Image (MRI) was normal and the physical findings were indicative of an acute episode, but nothing shocking. The physician was a colleague at the hospital. He knew me at my peak performance. He was aware of my capabilities and in taking the clinical view, I rested in the fact that my diagnosis could not be too terrible--his eyes spelled hope; my world was *not* going to end! As I left his office that day, I asked, "If I was your wife, what would you do?" He recommended counseling and the medical adjunct therapy (anti-depressant medication) prescribed by my psychiatrist. I remember during those months that the depth of my depression could only be addressed with the help of the medication. It lifted me to a place where the pastoral counselor could address the underlying issues. It is hard work, very hard work to put together the pieces of your life that you don't understand. I needed perspective, a new perspective. Until the new lens of faith helped me to order the events and my responses, I couldn't move on. And moving on is a choice, a clear choice with significant ramifications. It took love through the people God placed around me to heal.

I pondered the promise "made in the image of God"

"Your eyes saw my unformed body; all the days ordained for me were written in your book before one of them came to be." (Psalm 139.16)

This reflection reminded me of the eternality of my existence. John Wesley's sermon on the image of God states that we are infused with the power to 1) distinguish truth from falsehood; 2) endowed with a will, equally perfect; 3) responsible for our actions and 4) granted happiness as we draw closer to Him.

Happiness as part of the equation never stood out to me before. True joy begins to be emitted as we are drawn to Him and relinquish the past. My joy was exponential. I had long since given up worrying about people understanding my joy. It didn't matter. He was the source and I knew it. The key is humility, a knowledge of ourselves, a just sense of our condition. When we are enlightened by humility, we are immediately directed to reform our will. Becoming free from the law of sin and death, God restores us first to knowledge, then to virtue, to freedom and finally happiness. [3]

The background picture has now been painted for you. The worst had already taken place and the positive aspects of getting well were lining my path. I thanked God for people who care. I knew at that moment that there were no holds barred when our ultimate health is God's plan for us. Remembering my greatest gift, my faith, I held on to the assurance that my path would be made clear. In *Creation Spirituality: Liberating Gifts for the Peoples of the Earth*, Meister Eckhart states, as we learn the truth about our history and ourselves, we need to learn ways of letting go.[4]

I held on to Meister Eckhart's reminder to us that the seed of God is in us. *"Yet I had planted you a noble vine, a seed of highest quality."* *(Jeremiah 2:21)* "Origen, one of the great masters of the spiritual life, says that God Himself has sown this seed and inserted it and borne it. While this seed may be crowded, hidden away and never cultivated, it will still never be obliterated. It grows and shines, gives off light, burns, and is unceasingly inclined toward God."[5]

According to Saint Augustine, the stages of the inner and new person become apparent to others when: 1) A person lives according to the model of good and holy people, even though he or she still walks by leaning on chairs, walls and is nourished by milk. 2) When a person turns to external models, including good human beings, but also runs in haste to the teaching and advice of God, and the divine wisdom, turns his or her back to humanity, and their countenances to God, creep out of their mother's womb and smile at the heavenly Father. 3) When people more and more forsake their mothers and depart farther and farther from the womb, flee from care and throw off fear so that, even though they might, without annoyance, do evil and wrong to all others, they have no desire to do so. For they are so devoutly connected by love to God that He places and leads them in joy and sweetness and happiness to where everything is repellent to them that is dissimilar or foreign to God. 4) When people grow and become rooted in love and in God so that they are ready to take upon themselves every attack, temptation, vexation, and painful suffering willingly and gladly, eagerly and joyfully. 5) when people everywhere live at peace within themselves, quietly resting in the richness and abundance of the highest inexpressible wisdom. 6) when people are formed from and beyond God's eternity and attain a completely perfect forgetfulness of this temporary and passing life, when they are drawn and changed into the divine image, that is, when they have become children of God. Beyond this point there is no higher stage. Eternal rest and bliss are there, for the final goal of the inner persons and new persons is eternal life.[6]

I again asked myself "How will God use this to help me help others?" I innately knew that that was the plan, but I wasn't sure of the steps or their order. In her *"Walking Wounded or Wounded Healer"* article, Dr. Marion Conti-O'Hare expresses our need for meaning in our lives. With caring, compassion and empathy, our need for expression of the inner self is manifested when we are in contact with peers, students, patients and providers. By it's very nature, trauma has a cumulative effect.[7] The book goes on to describe the healers--whom they are and how they heal. The practitioners' attitude toward the healing process includes the expected level of healer and patient involvement.[8] Another factor is how healers perceive themselves and their motivation in pursuing particular healing practices. Nurses as wounded healers initially need to identify their fundamental beliefs about healing modalities along with the more significant aspect of engendering self-awareness.[9]

Dr. Conti-O'Hare describes differences in theoretical approaches:

Reductionist: usually associated with the Western model of medicine; applied when the human body or disease entity is viewed in terms of its smallest parts or forms. This view implies "causality" assuming that a new awareness of the health problem can be elicited and a definitive answer identified. In certain mental illnesses, for example, the cause appears to be at the cellular level, reflected by excesses or depletion of neurotransmitters in the brain that can affect emotions and behavior.

Holistic Perspective: Function oriented; the whole is greater than the sum of its parts. Humans and the environment are energy systems, which incorporate forces contributing to an every-changing diagnosis. Philosophically, its identification and treatment of patterns of harmony signal the awakening of innate health.

Osteopaths: believe that when restoration of the blood circulation occurs, the body can deal with disease its own way. They also hold that health and treatment of disease can be accomplished only through the study of the whole person in relation to the internal and external environments.

Homeopaths: Base their treatment on administering a drug resembling the disease itself. Within the healing spectrum, homeopathy extends beyond allopathic medicine, since it also includes spiritual beliefs. Edward Back (1931) has shown relationship between spirituality and drug treatment by introducing flower essences...remedies prepared only with water, sunlight and certain flowers or plants, 38 in total.

Mind and Faith Healing: requires the individual to believe that healing will occur. As such, mind-mediated healing takes place because of the confidence in the healer or healing method.

Psychic Healing: In ancient times, with the shamans, it sprang from the notion of healing emanating from a spiritual experience. (Stewart, 1990)

Energy Healing: belief that matter consists of energy with illness occurring as a imbalance in the human energy field produced by various internal or external causes. During the process, practitioners center themselves and use the natural sensitivity of the hands to assess the patterns of energy flow throughout the patient's body and to release blockages in the energy field.

Healing Touch: involves both contact and non-contact. Healing touch comes from the heart of the healer who transmits it to the person receiving help (Mentgen, 1996). Healing touch consists of six elements: 1) *awareness,* 2) *appraisal* (explore and evaluate awareness to consciousness). 3) *choosing*--how they respond to the disharmony, 4) *acceptance*--allowing energy flow to the disharmony, 5) *alignment*--integration of internal and external actions that support movement toward harmony and 6) *outcome*--harmony/wholeness.

Traditional Chinese Medicine: energizes the system through manipulations of the physical body, appropriate diet and exercise.

❋ ❋ ❋

Nursing is a discipline focused on assisting individuals, families and communities in attaining, re-attaining and maintaining optimal health and functioning. Modern definitions of nursing define it as a science and an art that focuses on promoting quality of life as defined by persons and families, throughout their life experiences from birth to care at the end of life.[10] Nurses acknowledge that the nursing profession is an essential part of the society from which it has grown. Authority for the practice of nursing is based upon social contract that delineates professional rights and responsibilities as well as mechanisms for public accountability. The practice of nursing involves altruistic behavior and is governed by a code of ethics. An extensive body of knowledge and associated skills are required in order to master the theory, practice and training in clinical skills. In all countries, nursing practice is defined and governed by law. National, state or territorial boards regulate entrance to the profession and nursing practice. It is a universal role appearing in some form in every culture.[11]

Increasingly, nurses have become aware that spiritual considerations cannot be ignored when adopting a holistic view of the person as the foundation of nursing practice. An important religious perspective of spiritual nursing care was the understanding of nursing being a calling, one where individuals cared for others out of a sense of duty and for the glory of God. Spiritual care was largely dependent on the skills of the nurse who must be able to discern a spiritual problem, design appropriate interventions and evaluate the outcomes (Mayer, 1992). Within the existential approach to spiritual care, all persons are valued as spiritual beings, regardless of their religious approach.[12] One goal of spiritual care is described as "self-in-relation" which is developed by "loving oneself, being in touch with others, caring, giving, being in love and developing one's relationships."[13] The role of the nurse is not to provide psychological or theological counseling but rather to be caring and present during the patient's search for meaning.

In looking back, I realized the steps that had taken place. When I came to the crisis point (requiring an intervention) I could no longer fend for myself. My own life resources were not enough. I needed help. What caused the stress response? It was a response that culminated from years of the practiced 'fight-flight-freeze' mode of living. Until God's light shined on the problem, I couldn't move forward. I needed every other person in my Sunday School class led by the Pastor and my husband, to give me new direction. I knew that nursing was my chosen path at that point. And with the fresh start of shed memories, I felt a new freedom with God that I had not known before. He does that, you know.

What was God calling me to next? First and foremost, it was, and still is, sharing the pain of that trauma. I am not alone. And neither are you.

SUMMARY
CHAPTER TEN - MOLDED FOR GOOD

An analogy is drawn between the process of pottery-making and our seemingly endless journey around the wheel of life. Such was the story of my life at the point that I now found myself. A series of automobile accidents and emotion-laden grief scenarios brought me to my knees.

Personally coping through an intervention, bar none, ranked as the most threatening experience I had ever known. Had my friends and the community of faith not been there, I would have been devastated. If the intervention had not proceeded well, I might still be suffering from the myriad of demons that clearly had a hold on my being. During the discovery phase of the Post Traumatic Stress Disorder, I was able to reveal the rape and subsequently begin to heal from the incident.

My counselors, mentors and friends surrounded me when I thought all hope was gone. I was re-introduced to my traumatic past and felt reassurance as God guided me. I recalled John Wesley's sermon on the image of God. The eternal nature that God instills in each of us gave me hope for the next step in my understanding. Meister Eckhart states that as we learn the truth about ourselves, we need to learn ways of letting go. In her book, *Walking Wounded or Wounded Healer,* Dr. Marion Conti-O'Hare describes the need for us to have meaning in our lives. She states that with caring, compassion and empathy, our need for self-expression is manifested when we are in contact with peers, students, patients and providers. Trauma, by its very nature, has a cumulative effect. Dr. Conti-O'Hare's description of *healers* and their attitudes toward the healing process follows.

Vocational choices, I believe, give us options that can play a vital role in helping us to heal. Healthcare workers, pastors and related caregivers often exhibit their spiritual gifts through an affinity for those are sick or injured.

QUESTIONS
CHAPTER TEN - MOLDED FOR GOOD

1. What does a "heavenward" focus mean to you? List three specific incidents when you looked to human understanding instead of praying it forth to God for an answer.

2. List two life experiences that God used to mold your character. Were either of these repetitions of an earlier lesson?

3. Meister Eckart's sermon addresses four key areas. Discuss your understanding of his point that man...

   a. Be free of himself and all things?

   b. Be formed again into a simple good?

c. Reflect on his soul's nobility?

d. Consider his divine nature?

4. God's promises are for us as well as our children. List two of God's promises that you have seen answered during your lifetime.

RESOURCES

1. O'Donnell, Michele (2005), *The God That We Have Created*, San Antonio: La Vida Press. Page 179

2. Ibid, Page 42

3. Internet Resource, John Wesley Sermon "The Image of God", The Green House, 9.09.2011

4. Fox, Matthew, (1980), *Meister Eckhart's Creation Spirituality in New Translation*, New York: Doubleday. Page 511

5. Ibid, Page 512

6. Ibid, Page 512

7. Conti-O'Hare, Marion, "Walking Wounded or Wounded Healer?" *Reflections on Nursing Leadership, First Quarter 2004* adapted from *The Nurse As Wounded Healer: From Trauma to Transcendence,* Sudbury, Massachusetts: Jones and Barltett Publishers, Incorporated. Page viii Preface

8. Ibid, page 17

9. Ibid, Page 18

10. Wikipedia, Internet encyclopedia, Nursing definition: http://en.wikipedia.org/nursing

11. Wikipedia, Internet Encyclopedia, http://en.wikipedia.org/nursing

12. Sawatsky, Rick and Barbara Pesut, (2007), *Attributes of Spiritual Care in Nursing Practice,* Albany: Trinity Western University Press. Page 21

13. Ibid, Page 22

CHAPTER ELEVEN
THE BOW ON THE PACKAGE

Consider the present--the package that's been sitting on the table until my birthday arrives. Never had I seen a package wrapped quite so beautifully. This hand-made paper represented hours of piecing and tearing, soaking and drying to build the paper's inner fibers; hand-picked mulberry leaves are a touch of nature that reminds me of my oneness with creation. Texture is also important. My sense of touch was intrigued by the surface of the paper as I pondered the hours of dying it must have taken to produce this bold slice of the rainbow. The artist in each of us can truly appreciate every step of the process.

I feel like that package--filled with potential. And yet no one has truly opened the layers that surround the "inner me," not even myself. My soul has been the nugget of gold that was placed there from the time of God's conception of me. What I do with that nugget is every bit a measure of where I am on this earthly journey called life. In learning about myself, I have learned about God. All that I take in has an effect on me, some experiences by my choice and others, not. My giftedness has allowed me to see bits of the greater plan, proven in countless ways through the years.

I know that I mirror my collective past, the joy-filled present and the hope of tomorrow. There is no escaping that past. It is part of that walk that tantalizes and transcends. As I have struggled during my valley or "down" times, I realize that I have never been alone and that nothing escapes God. My perception of the world around me is a measure of my individual past. You will have yours, coming piece-meal at certain teachable moments and revealed by the Holy Spirit. Your choice is to ignore or accept reality, to assess each situation and form a blueprint of your best future. I submit that the greatest gift we can give ourselves is the realization that only through God's grace are we formed, re-formed and transformed. It is only through the trials that we encounter that our potential is tapped. How else would we know where the 'edge of the envelope' lies? How else would we know the limits of our own human-ness and know when to rely on God instead of ourselves? Yes, we are called to go through trials but ultimately it is the grace of God that brings about transformation.

Because *"Thy word is a lamp unto my feet and a light unto my path." (Psalm 119:105)* I know I have a Creator who formed me in God's image. God's mercy, compassion and reassurance are confirmed in the First Book of Corinthians

> *"or do you not know that your body is the temple of the Holy Spirit which is in you, whom you have from God and you are not your own? For you were bought at a price; therefore, glorify God in your body and in your spirit which are God's."*
> *(1 Corinthians 6:19-20).*

God knew from the beginning of His plan for me—to this very time in history and in this very time with my family, my friends and my acquaintances.

"You formed my inward part; you knitted me together in my mother's womb. I praise you for I am wonderfully made. Wonderful are your works; my soul knows it very well. My frame was not hidden from you; when I was being made in secret, intricately woven in the depths of the earth. Your eyes saw my unformed substance; in your book were written every one of them, the days that were formed for me, when as yet there were none of them." (Psalm 139:13-16)

I know that I am created by Perfection itself and therefore, have the potential for true greatness. As a member of my generation, I am responsible and accountable to God. Deuteronomy spells out the reality that our love and obedience will be rewarded. Just as the Word becomes instilled in our hearts and hands, we then can translate that love to our children—whether waking or sleeping, walking or standing, it will gird us with God's strength to shelter and protect us.

"Therefore, you shall lay up these words of mine in your hearts and on your hands, and they shall be as frontlets between your eyes. You shall teach them to your children speaking of them when you sit in your house, when you walk by the way, when you lie down and you rise up. And, you shall write them on the doorposts of your house and on your gates, that your days and the days of your children may be multiplied in the land of which the Lord swore to your fathers to give them, like the days of the heavens above the earth." (Deuteronomy 11:18-21)

Knowing that God's nature is unchanging love, I have concluded that this journey is all about love. Love reaches out through the teachings, character and delivery by God's people; each day continues to be a *present* for each of us. As others are gifted to us, so we are gifted to each person and situation with whom we come in contact.

There is no limit to God's reach. When He introduced the Great Commandment *"Love the Lord your God with all your heart and with all your soul and with all your mind (Matthew 22:37)* He didn't say 'but not those in prison, not those that are homeless, not those that are mentally ill.' *"I was in prison and you visited me." (Matthew 25:36)*

He doesn't separate us as we separate ourselves. Until we internalize that truth, we will never realize the outreach that He truly has in mind. The prison walls of my mind held captive an untapped love. I knew innately that my strength came from above. I also knew that I would learn from above what must travel through my heart to others. God's love of Israel is my model for the love I can also expect. Whether part of the original tree or grafted into the tree, my promise is secure. Until we stretch our hand up to Him in prayer, we can never realize in our humanity, the growth that might be waiting to happen for others through us.

"And for their sake, He remembered His covenant, and relented according to the multitude of His mercies. (Psalm 106:45)

I know that I must never underestimate the power of human love in human relationships. Love, affection and belongingness reveal our human need for a stable, firmly based high level of self-respect and respect for others. Biblical wholeness spells out my ultimate progressions toward Body-Mind-Spirit balance. As a living temple, I must seek answers from the One who actively and intimately sculpts my form. Who else but a loving God prepares my way before I ever know it is planned.

"But the very hairs of your head are all numbered. Do not fear therefore; you are of more value than many sparrows." (Luke 12:7)

God's own words strengthen the power of love: *"If you love me, you will keep my commandments." (John 14:15)* I will recognize my "building up" by the harnessing of my will to God's design. *"Love is patient; love is kind." (1 Corinthians 13:4)* My protection is from above, *"putting on the breastplate of faith and love." (1 Thessalonians 5:8)*. Above all, I am no one's judge, for as the Word says *"And why do you look at the speck in your brother's eye but do not consider the plank in your own eye? (Matthew 7:3)* As I learned to "look" and not judge, I began to realize the goodness of God in each and every person. Not knowing the size, structure or angle of the "plank in my own eye' I realized that they, too, were on their own journey. How could I judge another human being when their path was totally unknown to me? God's goodness has many hues. If we weren't a rainbow of people, how could the spectrum of His love possibly be as brilliant!

Children learn what they live. My family surrounded me with love, nurture and a positive start in life. To love as Jesus loved paints a picture of total understanding. His perception, insight and total knowledge of human strengths and weaknesses allowed many lessons to be taught while in company with others and in many one-on-one encounters. Jesus routinely referred to a child in order to teach lessons. The disciples were driven by a need "to be somebody." According to the Book of John, every time this ambition surfaced, Jesus placed a child in their midst.[1]

The Spirit of Life is the Spirit of Love. The law of God is the Law of Love. Because love transforms, I am able to engender change. A solid foundation stood me well as steps of metamorphosis drew me closer to the realization of God's existence. Because of my stress behaviors of increased tension, inability to cope with the surroundings, verbal reminders of traumatic events (triggered by emotional red flags), I found myself spiraling back to darker times and found that my strength came not from me, but from the One who would show me steps back to health.

My path appeared to be opening up. As I returned to our congregation, opportunities for education, intervention and counseling became apparent. The birthing of a health ministry afforded a way for healthcare professionals to join forces and complement each others' work in preventative and wellness programs. Preparation of a preventative educational model addressing domestic violence enabled us to address family violence and abuse. The efforts mushroomed as resources were made available, women were educated and safe respite was made available for hurting victims. Little did I know that God would have in store for victims in Japan. Many years later, my husband and I opened a Spouse Abuse shelter at our military base. One by one, Jesus reached out to hurting people. One by one, I saw admission to a safe house as an invitation to offer Christ. *"I am the way, the truth, the life." John 14:6*

Only He has the answer for each of us. But first we may have to be removed from our current situation. Separation from the circumstances is sometimes necessary in order to hear the invitation. We must feel safe and protected to become aware of this new way of life.

Confusion still exists among the general population regarding self-esteem. The worldly view, of course, states that self-esteem is all-important. But self-esteem is not scriptural; it is of the flesh and is idolatry. We are to trust in God and not in ourselves. God's way for us is through biblical change. If we try to handle life's trials apart from God, wrong behaviors result as we respond to the old nature rather than the new nature. Our old nature must be reconciled as dead and therefore, not an option. God values each and every one of us, after all He created us. We have to realize our worth before we feel good enough to ask for help. Society has so engendered esteem as the central focus, we truly believe what the abuser says as they tear down our self-worth Learn to recognize it! Separate the lies from truth and begin with God's truth.

"Let not the food of pride come against me, and let not the hand of the wicked drive me away." (Psalm 36:11)

In order for Christian behavior to result, three steps are needed- 1) regeneration, 2) denial of self, and 3) a desire to please God in all things:

"...therefore, if anyone is in Christ, he is a new creation; old things have passed away; behold all things are new." (2 Corinthians 5:17)

The Book of Acts relays God's promises to Israel, extending today to all nations. A re-definition of the "people of God" results so that all peoples are included in God's work of salvation. This new picture of the people of God extends beyond Jewish and social categories of the past, with God creating a faithful community described in terms of God's presence, care for one another, unity among believers, and the unstoppable proclamation of the gospel.[2]

Reassurance and comfort are promised to me. *"Because the promise is for you, for your children."* *(Acts 2:39)* I believe God gifts the church with all the people necessary to accomplish the church's work. Understanding our part is critical to that completion.

> *"Having then gifts differing according to the grace that is given to us, let us use them; if prophecy, let us prophecy in proportion to our faith; or ministry, let us use it in our ministering; he who teaches, in teaching; he who exhorts in exhortation; he who gives, with liberality; he who leads, with diligence; he who shows mercy with cheerfulness."* *(Romans 12:6-8)*

A Covenant Promised and a Covenant Lived

God's covenant became my model. The trust and promise of permanent security is reinforced over and over in the Holy Bible. The initial TORAH (teaching) "that Moses commanded the Levites, who bore the Ark of the Covenant of the Lord states:

> *Take this Book of the Law and put it beside the Ark of the Covenant of the Lord Your God, that it may be there as a witness against you, for I know your rebellion and your stiff neck. If today, while I am yet alive with you, you have been rebellious against the Lord, then how much more after my death? Gather to me all the elders of your tribes, and your officers, that I may speak these words in their hearing and call heaven and earth to witness against them. For I know that after my death you will become utterly corrupt, and turn aside from the way which I have commanded you. And evil will befall you in the*

latter days, because you do evil in the sight of the Lord to provoke Him to anger through the work of your hands." *(Deuteronomy 31:25-29)*

This structures the government through worship and life of the people. The return of God's people to the Almighty's sovereignty brings the internal nature of the New Covenant.

"I will put My law in their minds and write it on their hearts, and I will be their God and they shall be my people." *(Jeremiah 31:33)*

My understanding of covenant relationships began when I realized God's loving relationship with me. Projected into present day, a streamlined approach has been developed which aggressively tackles related facets of a family crisis, one area at a time. Personally, I became aware of areas in my own life that needed focus, one being that of codependence. Just as my observations during childhood portrayed the female role I was to take in relationships, so I followed suit, neglecting personal health and wellness issues along the way.

As I have sought the proper role, surrender of my will to God's greater will has been the challenge. *"For God alone my soul waits in silence, for my hope is from Him."* *(Psalm 62:5)* Because God chose me, I can trust that I will grow and mature in His hands, for *"there is no fear in love."* *(1 John 4:18* Two natures exist within us. Upon my "rebirth" in Christ, I dedicated my life to becoming a servant to the people God chooses. My personal Lord and Savior became my model for healing and wholeness. Spiritual gifts surfaced that highlighted the shared teacher responsibility. In reaching out to others, my wounds were salved. Truly the Lord restored me in gentleness. *"Restore such a one in a spirit of gentleness."* *(Galatians 6:1)*

My calling has never changed. At times, it was more hidden than others, but, as God revealed the work to be done in me, my path became clear. The roller coaster of human events tumbled faster and faster until my personal capabilities were spent. I knew I needed God's help and direction. As I reoriented my vision toward kingdom promises, I experienced grace and truth for each step of the journey.

I likened my change to the process of pottery making-- digging, crushing, mixing, shaping and firing. Each process was a critical area of preparation for the next. Did my healing require help? You bet! Could I do it alone? Not at all. *"I am the vine, you are the branches; he who abides in Me and I in him bears much fruit; without me, you can do nothing." (John 15:1)* I witnessed the body of Christ in action. At my greatest vulnerability, the community gathered with love and secured my future through their prayers and presence. Timely intervention oriented me toward wholeness.

I rested in the knowledge that God held all the answers. As scripture was provided, the handling of life's problems became manageable steps: 1) Scripture resourced my deficits as I remembered that it is the sole legitimate standard by which life is measured. 2) the only authority on which to rely, 3) encouragement and hope are offered. Perseverance produced a pilgrimage to hidden areas of promise. Little did I know how God would use those areas when the timing was appropriate. Yet, only One knows whether you have come to the kingdom *"for such a time as this." (Esther 4:14)*

As my branches were trimmed, my roots sank deeper. Flexible and accepting by nature, I carried lessons learned during my desert wanderings forward as tools for the journey. I knew my identity in Christ clothed me with compassion, kindness, humility, gentleness and patience. Others were draw to God's love through me. Godly counsel and wisdom lighted my path as I reminded myself to rejoice in hope, be patient in trouble and steadfast in prayer. I marveled at God's variety in gifting fellow nurses in so many specialties. Margaret O'Brien's book "the Nurse with An Alabaster Jar" captures this thought in the Beatitudes for Nurses:

BEATITUDES FOR NURSES

...derived from Jesus' teaching during the Sermon on the Mount (Matthew 5:1-11)

> *Blessed are the nurse practitioners who care for the sick and the poor,*
>
> *For theirs is the kingdom of heaven.*

> *Blessed are the hospice nurses who mourn for patients lost,*
>
> *For they will be comforted.*

> *Blessed are the hospital staff nurses who minister to a wounded world,*
>
> *For they will inherit the land.*

> *Blessed are the parish nurses who advocate for marginalized parishioners,*
>
> *For they will inherit the land.*

> *Blessed are the home-care nurses who minister to the lonely and isolated,*
>
> *For they will be shown mercy.*

Blessed are the geriatric nurses who look tenderly upon the needs of frail elders,

For they will see God.

Blessed are the pediatric nurses who care for God's littlest ones,

For they will be called children of God.

Blessed are the missionary nurses who minister in distant lands,

For theirs is the kingdom of God.

Blessed are the military nurses who risk their lives in the line of duty,

For their reward in heaven will be great.[3]

SUMMARY
CHAPTER ELEVEN - THE BOW ON THE PACKAGE

Consider the package—the gift that is you. God created me as a unique gift with my heart the nugget of gold placed there from the time of His conception of me. All learning about myself is also my learning about God. My potential is only realized one level at a time, as the lens of faith which I have been granted, clears my vision of past events with more clarity and visioning from a new plateau toward the future.

Knowing that God's nature is unchanging love, I have come to the conclusion that this journey is all about love. Love reaches out through the teachings, character and delivery by God's people. I must never underestimate the power of human love in human relationships. The Beatitudes spell out rules for daily living. Because the world views self esteem as all important, we get mired in the "me" focus rather than focus on others. Self esteem is not scriptural; it is of the flesh. We are to trust in God and not ourselves. God's covenant became my model. The trust and promise of permanent security is reinforced over and over in the Bible; the challenge for me was surrendering my will to the Almighty's.

My calling has never changed. The roller coaster of life's challenges thwarted my path initially but as I re-oriented my vision toward kingdom promises, I experienced grace and truth in every step. I likened my change to the process of pottery-making—digging, crushing mixing, shaping and firing. Did I need help? You bet. I witnessed through the Body of Christ surrounding me, that change is possible. At my greatest vulnerability believers gathered with prayers and presence, orienting me toward wholeness.

My desert wandering produced tools for the journey. My identity in Christ clothed me with compassion, kindness, gentleness, humility and patience. Others were drawn to God's love through me. I might be a present to someone else.

QUESTIONS
CHAPTER ELEVEN - THE BOW ON THE PACKAGE

1. Love undergirds every gift of God. How is that gift of love presented in you?

2. How is each day a present for each of us?

3. Which of the Beatitudes is a challenge for you? Why?

4. What three relational entities reveal our human need for a stable, firmly based level of self- respect and respect for others?

5. What opportunities for education and intervention exist in your church? your community? Your workplace environment?

RESOURCES

1. Brennan, M. (1994), *Abba's Child*, Colorado Springs: Navpress. Page 95

2. The Wesley Study Bible, New Revised Standard Version (2009), Nashville: Abingdon Press. Page 1320

3. O'Brien, M. (2006) *The Nurse With An Alabaster Jar: A Biblical Approach to Nursing*, Madison: Nurse Christian Fellowship Press. Pg. 85

CHAPTER TWELVE
A TETHER THROUGH
THE TOUGH STUFF

Who or what is your tether? When the floor falls out from beneath you, who is there to give you that life-giving pull back to stability? Reality teaches us that life is a series of challenges and joys. Taken individually, our bodies respond to each event as we have been conditioned to do over time. As years of experience and responses have shown me, I am quick to respond and even quicker to escape into a self-protective, flight or freeze mode.

The telephone rang and my sister informed me that my stepdad had died. He had had a heart attack and went quickly, no more suffering with his emphysema and COPD. I scheduled my airline flight to Baltimore, to arrive the next day for the funeral. Mom was handling things pretty well, given her own cardiac issues and the shock of finding her husband dead in bed. She was happy to see me and welcomed someone to comfort her as the funeral arrangements were made. Long ago, both Mom and Dad decided on a mausoleum for burial and had pre-arranged the specifics. As I spoke at the funeral, I relayed my delight at age ten, of having a new Daddy. Ten years old is an important age to have 'family' mean completeness. My brother also spoke to the gathering relaying lessons learned and a positive reconciliation with Dad a few years prior.

So back to Texas I went, saddened for Mom but relieved as well. I had something to look forward to—I was going to spend New Years with my natural Dad on the west coast. I had not seen him in years and he was now suffering with cancer. I wanted to be there to cheer him up, to welcome in the new year with all its promises and new beginnings.

The telephone rang again. It was my sister saying that Mom was in the hospital with congestive heart failure. As usual, here I was right in the middle again—residing in Texas with Mom on the east coast and Dad on the west coast. My dream throughout my life was that I would get to see Mom and Dad in the same room to get a glimpse of what 'could have been' if things had all worked out. It was not meant to be.

Our son, Marcus and his family were already on the east coast, staying with in-laws and planning to see Mom. As my airplane taxied to take off that morning, my cell phone rang (long after the announcement to turn off cellular phones.) When I saw my son's name, I panicked; something had to be wrong. To make a long story short, he relayed the fact that my sister wouldn't allow him to see Mom in the hospital. I was at a loss. I encouraged him to meet me at the airport when I arrived and we would see Mom together. In mid-flight that day, I knew Mom had died. My spirit responded and I was at peace with God's plan.

Mom's funeral, to say the least, was full of deep emotion. All the years of struggle, all the years of wonder about what could have been were suddenly cut short. The trip to the funeral home to see her left me 'frozen in time.' She was at peace—at least I knew that the peacemaker in our family would finally be at peace herself. She was now with Our Lord, and what a comfort that was.

The family dynamics all came rushing back. With my brother now present with his family, the flood of decisions regarding the funeral provided a temporary focus. Our son and his family arrived and my job became ultra-important. How could I guide him through the flood of emotions that he himself experienced? You can't bring back the years spent away—you can't re-connect when the opportunities are gone. But I encouraged him to write Mom a letter and I would place it in the casket with her. Fortunately, all of his memories of Grandma were positive. She had cared for him albeit at a distance and through many delightful telephone conversations connected with generational stories and love. Mom was the kindest, gentlest person I ever knew.

The funeral home was flooded with those who knew Mom and loved her as much as we did. Her positive spirit transcended any negative that came her way, clearly because her connection to God remained solid and strong. Given all that she experienced in her lifetime — four children, eldercare of a mother-in-law for more than 20 years, business success and losses, it is a wonder she remained as solid as she did. She was definitely a witness to God's strength poured through her every action.

My personal trial was not over yet however. When I returned home after the funeral, I wanted to check on my west coast Dad. After a call to my brother, I learned that he too had died the same day, seven hours earlier than Mom. I melted into my seat and thanked God for answering my lifelong prayer. My only wish was that my parents be in the same room sometime during my life. Now they finally were.

"My Father's house has many rooms; if that were not so, would I have told you that I am going there to prepare a place for you?" (John 14:2)

With this chapter of my life now closing, I seemed strangely settled. The reality of being the oldest one in the family seemed a somewhat foreboding reality. It was now up to me to carry on the traditions and lifeblood that had started in our home to future generations. I remembered the feelings as I left the nest for college, my first exposure to the outside world. After graduation, I moved back home to known territory for my first year of work. My real awakening came, however, when I moved to Florida and my first active duty assignment. That was truly "away."

As I settled into the work world, I began to see how truly big the world was. Questions that rose to the surface were those dealing with my own inadequacies. I already felt strong and capable, but didn't know how to mend the severed relationships in the family. When do I stop trying? Should I? What would Jesus do here? I kept remembering all the times that I reached out to siblings with no response. It was always me extending the arm of connection; no one ever called me except to deliver bad news. The reality that our relationship may have been for Mom's sake really hurt. What do I do now, Lord?

Because our gifts and talents are so much a part of who we are, the way we translate God's love to others will be just as unique. God's love is the fulfillment of the law. When we are perfected in love, we have been perfected in all. Our actions will reveal the choices we have made. Think of children and then think of yourself as a child. It is the reinforcement of positive behaviors that will inspire us. After all, our potential is most often seen by those who live with us and observe our everyday behaviors. Generation upon generation journey in the world acculturated to believe the teachings of that time and place. A nurturing mother is the one identity to whom the child clings. The Beatitudes *(Matthew 15:3-12)* list eight simple virtues taught by Christ. A way of life is offered that promises eternity in the kingdom of heaven Matthew 18:3 tells us

"Truly I say to you, unless you turn and become as little children, you will by no means enter the kingdom of heaven."

Jesus often used children as examples, children because they become the leaders of adults. They are less jaded in their thinking, more prone to listen and quite open in matters of the heart. Love is imprinted, implanted. The spiritual aspect of our being transcends all others when we are in balance. Our decisions are clear, our ethics are upheld and the quality of our character is apparent since we are accountable not just to our profession or family, but more importantly, to God.

I know that I must never underestimate the power of human love in human relationships. Love, affection, and belongingness reveal our human need for a stable, firmly based, high level of self-respect and respect for others. I will recognize my building up by the harnessing of myself to God's design.

A Note About Sin

Each of us defines sin for ourselves, but I want to address it from a generational point of view. Sin is real. Sin is powerful and is in fact, deadly. But don't give sin more power than it deserves. Yes, we should take it seriously, but know that a far greater power is here in the world--the power of the Gospel of Jesus Christ. J.D. Walt says, "Most of us have been discipled along the way to believe in the gravitational pull of sin. Sin--Confess--Repent--Repeat. This leads not only to low self esteem, but to an anemic perspective of the power of God."

John 10:10: The thief comes to kill and destroy, but I have come that they may have life and have it more abundantly."

Always remember, "You are a new creation in Christ. The old has passed away and the new has come." (1 Corinthians 5:17)

So you might ask, "How do I break the power of sin?" I submit that it is by knowing the Healer. Only in Jesus Christ have we been freed and cleansed of any past sin; by our repentance we are called to His side to walk through the healing steps. Listen again to the Creator's touch in creating our bodies.

Oswald Chambers in his October 5th meditation, describes it this way:

"Sin is a thing I am born with and I cannot touch it; God touches sin in redemption. In the cross of Jesus Christ God redeemed the whole human race from the possibility of damnation through the heredity of sin. God nowhere holds man responsible for having the heredity of sin. The condemnation is not that I am born with the heredity of sin but if, when I realize Jesus Christ came to deliver me from it, I refuse to let Him do so. From that moment I begin to get the seal of damnation."

"And this is the judgment" the critical moment...that the light is come into the world and men loved the darkness rather than the light. *(John 3:19)*

If Jesus is to regenerate me, what is the problem He is up against? I have a heredity I had no say in; I am not holy, nor likely to be; and if all Jesus can do is tell me I must be holy, His teachings plant despair. But if Jesus is the re-generator, one who can put into me His own heredity of holiness, then I begin to see what He is driving at. The moral transaction on my part is agreement with God's verdict on sin in the Cross of Jesus Christ. The New Testament teaching about regeneration is that when a man is struck by a sense of need, God will put the Holy Spirit into his spirit and his spirit will be energized "until Christ is formed in you." When I reach the frontier of need and know my limitations, Jesus says "Blessed are you." But God cannot help me until I am conscious that I need it."

MY WAKE UP CALL — A Turning Point

It was a Thursday afternoon. I was getting my fingernails manicured at a beauty shop near our home. The lady had gone to the back of the shop for a moment and I noticed a book on the corner of the table. It's title had something to do with salvation. Was I saved? Was I sure? A flood of guilt washed over me and I wasn't sure. She took one look at me and noticed that I was visibly shaken. "Are you OK? she said."

"I'm not sure" I replied.

"What's going on in your life right now? Would you like to come back to the back and pray when we're finished?" I prayed with her and received some Godly instruction. I was preparing to go on a retreat and did not know how to prepare for it. She encouraged me to take only my Bible to my favorite spot by Canyon Lake; my goal was to pray and center myself for the events God had in store. As I prayed at the lake, I pled with God to show me the way. Pouring my heart out to Him was the most natural thing I knew to do. He led me through the Bible, teaching me where to look and why. After a time, I woke through the tears and noticed that I had slid off the rock where I sat. My knees were locked in place and I couldn't get up. As I looked to my left, I saw a HUGE goose not 18 inches away from me. His eyes told the story. God wanted me to know that I was not alone. He sent a comforter.

FEAR

What do you do when fear enters the scene? Our first response is our body's physical reaction. It's the fight — flight — or freeze scenario. Fear creates this response because we are human and our senses were placed in us for safety and protection. But fear creates spiritual amnesia; it dulls our miracle memory. When fear shapes our lives, safety becomes our God. The fear-filled life cannot love deeply. Love is risky. Those fearful cannot give to the poor because there is no guarantee of return.

If we medicate fear with angry outbursts, drinking binges, sullen withdrawals, we exclude God from the solution and exacerbate the problem. We allow anxiety to dominate and define us. Christ issued a blessing before one was requested, *"Take courage, my son; your sins are forgiven."* (Matthew 9:2)

Before Jesus healed the body He treated the soul; He was thinking about our deepest fear—fear of failing God. To sin is to disregard God, ignore His teachings, deny His blessings. Fear, mismanaged leads to sin; sin leads to hiding. We have all sinned, not hidden in the bushes necessarily, but in 88-hr workweeks, temper tantrums, religious busy-ness. Jesus loves us too much to leave us in doubt about His grace. His *"perfect love expels all fear"* (John 4:18). Legitimate concern can morph into toxic panic. Inoculate yourself inwardly to face your fears outwardly; cast all your care on Him.

Let's talk about family. Since our nuclear families are our first training ground, it is important to understand the effect that all those behaviors have had in our past, our present, and in our future should we choose to continue the responses. All of us want to protect our children. Our parents wanted to protect us. It's easy to say now that I should have prayed more then. Now we can look at our 20/20 hindsight and know that all children need to be raised in the greenhouse of prayer. It is incumbent upon us to instill in our children a sense of their place in this world and a heavenly place in the next. As a grandma now, it is increasingly apparent to me that lessons learned by the grandchild, coping mechanisms taught at the earliest opportunity, are the best defense we can instill in the next generation.

Storms are not an option but fear is! Dr. David Jeremiah gives the following visual comparison. "Consider the two ends of the spectrum between prudence and paranoia. Prudence wears a seat belt — paranoia avoids cars. Prudence washes with soap; paranoia avoids human contact. Prudence saves for old age; paranoia hoards even the trash. Prudence prepares and plans; paranoia panics. Prudence calculates the risk and takes the plunge; paranoia never enters the water."

Jesus made his fears public. He *"offered up prayers and petitions with loud cries and tears to the One who could save Him from death." (Hebrews 5:7)*

Evildoers have less chance of hurting you if you aren't already a victim. I found myself watching the world (and the evil in it) contrasted with the promises of Jesus and what we are called to do in looking to Him for the answer. I remembered the Scripture

"When my Father sends the Advocate as my representative, the Holy Spirit, He will teach you everything and will remind you of everything I have told you. I am leaving you with a gift—peace of mind and heart. And the peace I give the world cannot give. So don't be troubled or afraid." (John 14:26-27)

In this Scripture, Jesus is preparing His disciples for His earthly departure. Christ provided courage through community; He dissipated doubt through fellowship and never distributed all knowledge to one person. "Jesus distinguishes His peace for the world's peace. He reassures the disciples and now reassures us, in His subordination to the Father. He invokes the distinction between the time of His ministry when He is speaking and the time after His death when they may understand and believe." Remember, courage is fear that has said its prayers. God chooses to be known to us so that we may not be afraid of the wrong thing. Fear of the Lord is recognition that we are not God.

Definition: Fear is an emotion induced by a threat, real or perceived, which causes a change in brain and organ function and ultimately a change in our behavior. It is a vital response to physical or emotional danger—if we didn't feel it, we couldn't protect ourselves from legitimate threats. Traumas or bad experiences can trigger a fear response within us. It is critical, therefore, to expose the fear to move beyond it.

What fears kept you up at night as a child? In recent years? What emotions and physical reactions typically accompany your experience of fear? What do your past and present fears reveal about your values? Desires? Dreams?

When I ask "What are you afraid of" I am really asking.... what immobilizes you? What steals your joy, destroys your hope? robs you of sleep? On a spiritual level, what prevents you from entrusting your life wholly to God? Scripture commands us more than 300 times NOT to fear.

Fear not, for I am with you; Be not dismayed, for I am your God. I will strengthen you, yes I will help you. I will uphold you with My righteous right hand. (Isaiah 41:10:)

"So He said "Come" and when Peter had come down out of the boat, he walked on the water to go to Jesus. But when he saw that the wind was boisterous, he was afraid; and beginning to sink he cried out saying, "Lord, save me." (Matthew 14:29-30)

Fear of Failure...without taking risks, you are already defeated. Consider Moses in the "call" narratives.

Then Moses said to the Lord, "O my Lord, I am not eloquent, neither before nor since You have spoken to your servant; but I am slow of speech and slow of tongue. He said, O my Lord, please send by the hand of whomever else you may send. (Exodus 4:10,13)

The Bible is your launch-pad for encouragement and instruction. When I need encouragement, I remember God's encouragement to David in Psalm 37:

"Do not fret because of the wicked, do not be envious of wrongdoers, for they will soon fade like the grass and wither like the green herbs. Trust in the Lord and do good for you will live in the land and enjoy security. Take delight in the Lord and He will give you the desires of your heart." (Psalm 37:1-4)

Though it appears, at times, that the wicked appear to be living the good life, I am reminded that patience and trust are the keys to waiting on God's timing for their judgment. The wicked and their acts will not last forever.

When I need instruction, I remember that I am not in this life alone. God promises His help through others as we experience the Body of Christ in human form. *"As iron sharpens iron, so one person sharpens another." (Proverbs 27:17)* Maybe my perception of being corrected is really instructive, not meant to hurt me but to help me. Receiving and assimilating discipline takes time. Information needs processing as we let the watering of God's Words soak deep into our roots. Unless and until that happens, the heartbeat of new life cannot take form.

Fear of Depression

What should be your first course of action? Know your enemy! Because we are holistic beings (body-mind-spirit) depressed people suffer not just in spirit, but also in body. We become ill more often, lose energy for everyday life and fall into lethargy or escape into sleep. Jesus Christ is the ultimate antidote to depression and fear of depression. If we maintain faith and hope, losses can be restored.

The Sword of the Spirit—the Word of God is the offensive weapon in the Christian's spiritual armor. In times of spiritual warfare, it is the only way to counter the lies Satan always tells. When Jesus stood up to Satan He said,

> *"You are of your father the devil, and the desires of the father you want to do. He was a murderer from the beginning and does not stand in the truth, because there is no truth in him. When he speaks a lie he speaks from his own resources for he is a liar and the father of it."(John 8:44)*

Isolation: If we are doing what God calls us to do, we'll always experience interference in one form or another. The greater our commitment to Christ, the more we will be disconnected from the crowd. We can't worry about what others think or do. Encounters with true isolation are acutely painful. They affect us emotionally, mentally, spiritually and even physically. How do I win? Find companionship, compassion, courage. Find Christ!

Disease: The truth is, we all fear disease. Let's face it, even if you don't face a major catastrophic event, one of the following 4 physical events will most likely lead to our death...heart attack, cancer, diabetes or stroke. For most of us, illness will be the vehicle by which we transition to eternity. Disease is inevitable but it doesn't have to control us or drive us into panic.

What is the sickest you have ever been? How have you experienced turmoil and disruption because of it? Serious illness takes an emotional toll as well. The first thing to do is get involved in our healing. Healing builds our faith by giving us hope. As a first step talk to God about it; ask Him for guidance and healing. The cycle of reaching to God in prayer (1 Thessalonians 5:17 *"Pray without ceasing"*), listening for guidance and doing all that we can in our human capacity narrows the gap between our illness or injury and asking God's help to heal us. In so doing, we are reminded not to fear. Then remember *"For God has not given us a spirit of fear, but of power and of love and of a sound mind."* *(2 Timothy 1:7)* Gaining a sound, centered mind is not as difficult as you think. When we read Scripture deeply, thoughtfully and openly we allow the Holy Spirit to whisper new strength into our thoughts. Count your blessings, continue your work and consider your future.

Fear of Death

"Yea, though I walk through the valley of the shadow of death, I will fear no evil; for you are with me; Your rod and Your staff, they comfort me." (Psalms 23:4)

How does the reality that you are already experiencing eternal life influence your perspective on death? Physical death literally means separation. In physical death the Spirit leaves the body and moves either into the presence of God or isolation from Him. Spiritual death. Romans 6:23 tells us *"For the wages of sin is death but the gift of God is eternal life in Christ Jesus our Lord."* Adam and Eve didn't die physically when they ate the forbidden fruit although their bodies began the process of death at that moment. But they did experience spiritual death immediately after their sin. Thankfully, our spiritual death doesn't have to remain a permanent condition.

For Christians, the many forms of death are temporary. It is appropriate for us to mourn the death of our loved ones and even feel apprehension about our separation, but in the end we hold fast to the knowledge that Christ has already secured our ultimate victory over the grave.

Fear of God

When we look to Scripture, fear is an essential element in our relationship to God. We can't move forward as members of His kingdom until we gain a realistic understanding of His plan in relation to our weakness.

There are two important aspects to fearing God—First, profound awe...the starting point of our relationship with Him. Then comes astonished devotion. Once the proper foundation is established, the distance between His holiness and our sinfulness, we begin to balance our fear and dread with something new. We have a new connection. We realize that God's Word, His law, is a love letter to us. It is meant for our good and His glory. Because He loves us so much, the saturation of His very being is a total gift from heaven every time we recognize it. Sometimes that downpour is in the form of a shower, sometimes a rainstorm and sometimes a hurricane. Regardless, it's all His created weather. Our response is what we will for our future.

Children of God can now live with absolutely no fear of God's wrath. Because our sins have been forgiven and the penalty has already been paid through the death and resurrection of Jesus Christ, we have an assurance engraved in eternity. Maintain a healthy fear of God. Fear God because of WHO He is, WHAT He has done, and what He CONTINUES to do today. There is no one like Him. There is no one who offers His promises of provision, protection, prolonged days or privilege. Don't sell yourself short. He has placed you today in this very spot to launch your learning to the next level.

MY SPIRITUAL JOURNEY

God has truly blessed me. In my seven decades, He has nurtured, guided, cared for and protected me in any and all circumstances. From childhood, I knew and loved God, always seeking Him and feeling totally at peace inside our Lutheran church. It was there that I got in tune with my artistic side and began to appreciate the giftedness He had placed within me. It was through Mom's nurture (mother of four children, church pianist and accomplished seamstress) that I learned the most about expressing my inner joy and relating everything I saw to Our Creator. Born with boundless energy, I soaked up all the lessons she spread before me, always harkening back to her encouraging phrase, "Donna, There is nothing in the world that you can't do if you put your mind to it."

The Air Force provided a panorama of opportunities. In helping the sick, I learned that my spirit grew. I saw the underlying need in patients and spoke to that when I cared for them. God is always their real need. I began to study the nurses and personalities--nurses have one foot in the sciences and one in the arts. God created us with five senses but my view of the senses is much deeper; I believe we only see only a glimpse of what is truly there. I believe we are affected by our leaders, affected by our coworkers, and yes, even affected by every responses to or from our patients or contacts. It is all human learning. Our bodies respond to others; we were made to respond. But never forget that our body keeps the score. Countless research studies have proven that changes occur, even to the level of our DNA. What humans sometimes mean for harm, God can reverse and heal.

In the church, in my nursing directors' jobs and in my consulting, I saw how strengths/weaknesses affect each and every relationship. Until we understand our 'giftedness', I don't believe we know how to develop our dreams. Meister Eckhart understood 'God within us.' I think he knew how God yearns to reach others--through us but more importantly through groups or families of us who reach out in unique and caring ways.

Teaching and leadership are at the summit of my mountain of gifts. Now I find myself blessed with grandchildren that are so talented and fragile I want to surround them with all that God has to offer. I am instilling in them a sensitivity to the Spirit that I didn't learn until much later. My Walk to Emmaus at age 50 opened my eyes to the reality of God's presence in everything I touched. My worst fault at that time was rushing ahead of His plan for me. Once I learned the rhythm of the Spirit, I tied my prayer life to more closely reflect His plan. If it wasn't supposed to be, I asked God to remove it--over and over. Just a few years ago I knew I was supposed to start a children's choir at our Austin church. I did the groundwork, researched the programs and worked with the Music Director to bring it to fruition. Today the Cherubs praise God at their peak of three to five-year old voices. God led me to dance. In our San Antonio church, liturgical dance was introduced. I learned prayer in a new dimension.

On the intellectual side, I knew my easy connection to people made me a natural to teach Bible study. My spirit grew. Christian fellowship provides the most natural environment for true accountability and growth. Bible studies vary with groups and churches. Preparation for my teaching is critical to the overlying principle that God wants us to learn from Him, to turn to Him. The safety and security of the study group harkens back to John Wesley's small group experience (bands). We are meant to grow spiritually and meant to help and hold each other accountable. As adults and as our nuclear family wanes, our new Christian fellowship is presented.

I see God's timing as very ordered. The sudden loss of three parents' lives in a three-week period, totally closed a chapter in my life. I took myself back to the first, then the second, then the third death, and tried to make sense of it. Was there a purposeful order? There were no "additional threads" to figure out, no more guessing about the past, or motives or the realities that played out in our families. It was over. How had my preconceived ideas about God's healing open and closed so many chapters in an instant? There is wisdom in opening new doors, doors to new family and those that may not be our blood but may just be the life-giving blood that God intended.

I think of teachers, mentors and inspirers. Each of them, in retrospect, fed me with the same enthusiasm that Mom ignited every time she saw my potential. Each of them saw in me something that I did not see in myself yet. They saw my God-given gifts and knew, if cultivated, could become a beacon of light to those who needed my help. How treasured our existence becomes when we realize the positive influence we can create, just by being who we are.

Mom was a peacemaker, first and foremost. She held the family together through thick and thin. Whatever challenges were presented, she sifted through with Godly intuition and presented viable options for pursuit of our plans. The telephone call that I made to her from college is a good example. I was totally discouraged because I did not have straight A's in my Pre-Med College courses. Her response was totally positive, "Do you think you still want to work with patients?" she said. Yes was my answer. What about becoming a nurse? I was so shocked that I hadn't thought of it, it gave me new inspiration. There was something I could do...and do well...I thought. Boy, was she right.

Seasons change in our lives. Now in my seventh decade, my perspective has changed a bit. I can see my right and my wrong decisions more clearly. I can direct my future steps around the known land mines that Satan presents. I believe God calls us in His eternal invitation to turn again to Him, draw us closer, give us renewed vision with an understanding look at our past, and more importantly, a clearer vision of His lighted signposts for our future. *"In his heart a man plans his course but the Lord establishes his steps."* (Proverbs 16:9)

SUMMARY
CHAPTER TWELVE - A TETHER THROUGH THE TOUGH STUFF

Who, or what is your tether? For me it was, and is God.... God's love extended through my Mom. That lifeline was tested to the limits as I experienced three deaths in three weeks--my step-dad, my dad and then my mom. Spread across three areas of the country, our families converged for the funerals and the tough issues surrounding the grief process. Immediate family and generational family needs took center stage. In all my experiences of death (i.e.: hospitals, nursing homes, church) I had never experienced the flood of emotions resulting from unresolved family issues. The doors that had been blocked for healing were suddenly a floodgate of guilt, blame and questioning.

Paramount in this flood of emotion was my heartfelt praise for my Mom, her conviction in love, strength in conflict and determination to turn everything into a good, positive future. Looking back, the generations in our family had dealt with similar positives and negatives, not unlike most families I would guess. Mom had the strength of a lion and the gentleness of a lamb.

As I considered my own spiritual journey, the effects of sin and fear crept to the surface as major roadblocks. At age 50 and my re-birth in Christ I had a new vision of God's plan for me. As He led me through my journey I realized that there was nothing I needed to fear. I had already dealt with it--the fears of defeat, depression, isolation, disease and death. God was and still is-- my Shepherd.

Lessons ranged from my youth through military service, my retirement, continued education and current ministries. God's giftedness to me has always drawn others to seek Him through me. As my footprints continue, may I join the throngs of seekers, ready for a new heart.

QUESTION
CHAPTER TWELVE - A TETHER THROUGH
THE TOUGH STUFF

1. Have you ever been struck with a sudden loss or death of a loved one? How did you cope?

2. Define 'sin' as you know it today. Do you believe that unforgiven sin has power over your actions?

3. Fear is an emotion induced by a threat, real or perceived. Relate one of your most fear-filled moments and how you coped. Did you turn to God for help?

4. Of these six fears (defeat, depression, isolation, disease, death, God) what are the top two that you deal with today? List three positive responses, given your new learning.

5. Different decades of our lives teach us valuable lessons. What is the greatest lesson you have learned from God's reassurance through Scripture?

RESOURCES

1. Electronic: Walt, J. D., Seedbed Daily Text, jd.walt@seedbed. com

2. Chambers, Oswald (1963), My Utmost For His Highest: Classic Edition, Grand Rapids: Discovery House Publishers. October 5th meditation.

3. Jeremiah, David (2013), What Are You Afraid Of? Facing Down Your Fears With Faith, Carol Stream: Tyndale Publishers.

4. Wikipedia : Fear definition

5. Mays, James L. Editor, HarperCollins Bible Commentary, Harper: San Francisco, 1988, Pages 978-9.

6. Van Der Kolk (2014), Blackstone Publishing, Gildan Media Audiobooks, The Body Keeps the Score.

BIBLIOGRAPHY

Beattie, M. (1987). *Codependent No More: How to Stop Controlling Others and Start Caring for Yourself*, San Francisco: Harper and Row, Publishers.

Birkman, R. (2002) *A Man of Understanding*, Houston, TX: Birkman Internaitonal, Incorporated.

Carnes, P. (1960). *The Betrayal Bond: Breaking Free of Exploitive Relationships*, Deerfield Beach: Heath Communications.

Chambers, O. (1992). *My Utmost for His Highest*, Grand Rapids: Discovery House Publishers.

Conti-O'Hare, M. (2002). *The Nurse as Wounded Healer: From Trauma to Transcendence*, Sudbury: Jones & Bartlett Publishers.

Coogan, M. (1998). *The Oxford History of the Biblical World*, New York: Oxford University Press.

Fox, M. (1980). *Breakthrough: Meister Eckhart's Creation Spirituality in New Translation*, New York: Image Books/ Doubleday.

Fox M. (1998). *Creation Spirituality: Liberating Gifts for the Peoples of the Earth*, New York: Oxford University Press.

Goleman, D. (1995). *Emotional Intelligence,* New York: Bantam Books.

Grenz, S., D. Guretzki and C. Nordling (199). *Pocket Diagnosis of Theological Terms,* Downers Grove: Intervarsity Press.

Gurian, M. (2002). *The Soul of the Child: Nurturing the Divine Identity of Our Children,* New York: Atria Books.

Jacobson, M. (2006). Nutrition Action Health Letter: *Six Arguments for a Greener Diet, Vol. 24:1,* Evangelical Press.

Jamison, S. (2007). Journal of Christian Nursing, January-March. *Called to Teach: How Did Jesus Teach?* Downers grove: Intervarsity Christian Press.

Laub, D. & Poell, D. (1995). *Art and Trauma, International Journal of Psychoanalysis,* 76 912), 991-1005.

Manning, B. (1994). *Abba's Child.* Colorado Springs: Navpress Books and bible Studies.

Marill, M. (2001). *Experiencing Biblical Wholeness,* Columbus: Brentwood Christian Press.

Mayo Clinic (2007. *Domestic Violence Toward Women,* Internet Resource.

McGinn, B. (1986). *Teacher and Preacher,* New York: Paulist Press.

Murray, A. (1981). *With Christ in the School of Prayer,* Kensington: Whitaker House.

Nolte, Dorothy Law (1972). *Children Learn What They Live,* New York, New York.

O'Brien, M. (2006). *The Nurse With An Alabaster Jar: A Biblical Approach to Nursing,* Madison: Nurse Christian Fellowship Press.

O'Donnell, M. (2005). *Of Monkeys and Dragons-Freedom From the Tyranny of Disease,* San Antonio: LaVida Press.

O'Donnell, M. (2005). *The God That We Have Created,* San Antonio: LaVida Press.

Osbeck, K. (2002). *Amazing Grace: 366 Inspiring Hymn Stories,* Grand Rapdids: Kregel Publishers.

Richards, L. (1987). *The Teacher's Commentary,* Wheaton: Scripture Press Publications.

Sawatsky, R. and B. Pesut (2007). *Attributes of Spiritual Care in Nursing Practice,* Albany: Trinity Western University Press.

Sorajjakool, S. (2007). *When Sickness Heals: The Place of Religious Belief in Healthcare,* Philadelphia: Templeton.

United States Food and Drug Administration, Department of Health and Human Services, Center for Food Safety and

Applied Nutrition, (2006). *Fresh and Frozen Seafood, Selecting and Serving it,* August, Washington: United States Printing.

Vos, H. (1999). *New Illustrated Bible Manners and Customs.* Nashville: Thomas Nelson Publishers.

Wangerin, W. (2003). *Little Lamb Who made Thee?,* Grand Rapids: Zondervan Publishers.

Westberg, G. (1990). *The Parish Nurse: Providing a Minister of Health for Your Congregation,* Minneapolis: Augsberg Fortress.

Whitaker, R. and J. Kohlenberger III (2000). *The Analytical Concordance to the NRSV of New Testament,* Grand Rapids: William B. Erdman Publishers.

ELECTRONIC

Aquarian Gospel of Jesus Christ (1920). http://www.sacred-texts.
com/chr/agic/index.html

Harvard medical School (2005). The Brazelton Institute, *The
Newborn Behavioral Observation System: What Is It?* http://
ww.brazeltoninstitute.com/clnbas.html

Mayo Clinic, *Domestic Violence Toward Women.* http://www.
clinic/health/domestricviolence

St. Gregory of Nyssa, The Lord's Prayer and the Beatitudes,
Ancient "Christian Writer Series", Hahwah: Paulist Press. http://
www.jesuschristsaciro.net/Beatitudes.html

Wikipedia (2006). http://en.wikipedia.org/wiki/domesticviolence

Wikipedia (2006). http://en.wikipedia.org/domesticviolence/
physicaltrauma

Wikipedia (2003). http://en.wikipedi.org/wiki/Eckhart

Wikipedia (2006). http://en.wikipedia.org/wiki/Jung

Wikipedia (2006). http://en.wikipedia.org/wiki/nursing

Wikipedia (2006). http://en.wikipedia.org/wiki/Piaget

Wikipedia (2006). http://en.wikipedia.org/wiki/potential

SCRIPTURE INDEX

CHAPTER ONE

CHAPTER TWO

Pg 15 "you shall therefore lay up these words of mine in your heart and in your soul and you shall bind them as a sign on your hand and they shall be as front lets between your eyes. You shall teach them to your children, talking of them when you are sitting in your house and when you are walking by the way, and when you lie down and when you rise. You shall write them on the doorposts of your house and on your gates, that your days and the days of your children may be multiplied in the end that the LORD swore to your fathers to give them, as long as the heavens are above the earth." (Deuteronomy 11:18-21)

Pg 15 "For you formed my inward parts; you knitted me together in my mother's womb. I praise you, for I am fearfully and wonderfully made. Wonderful are your works, my soul knows it very well. My frame was not hidden from you, when I was being made in secret, intricately woven in the depths of the earth. Your eyes saw my unformed substance, in your book were written, every one of them, the days that were formed for me, when as yet there were not of them." (Psalm 139:13-16)

Pg 17 It was you, God, who "fashioned me in my mother's womb." (Psalm 139:13)

Pg 21 "Or do you not know that your body is the temple of the Holy Spirit who is in you, whom you have from God, and you are not your own? For you were bought at a price; therefore, glorify God in your body and in your spirit, which are God's." (1 Corinthians 6:19-20)

Pg 22 "but let a man examine himself, and so let him eat of the bread and drink of the cup. For he who eats and drinks in an unworthy manner, eats and drinks judgment to himself, not discerning the Lord's body." (1 Corinthians 11:28-29)

Pg 23 "Thy kingdom is not of this world," (John 18:36)

Pg 23 "And he said to them, 'Take nothing for the journey, neither staffs nor bag, nor bread, nor money; and do not have two tunics apiece. Whatever house you enter, stay there, and from there depart. And whoever will not receive you, when you go out of that city, shake off the very dust from your feet as testimony against them.'" (Luke 9:3-5)

Pg 23 "but the very hairs on your head are all numbered. Do not fear, therefore; you are of more value than many sparrows." (Luke 12:7)

Pg 24 It was you, God, who "fashioned me in my mother's womb." (Psalm 139:13)

CHAPTER THREE

Pg 27 "And for their sake He remembered His covenant; and relented according to the multitude of His mercies." (Psalm 106:45)

Pg 29 "Love the Lord your God with all your heart." (Matthew 22:37)

Pg 29 "If you love me, you will keep my commandments." (John 14:15)

Pg 29 "Love is patient; love is kind" (1 Corinthians 13:4)

Pg 29 "Love never ends" (1 Corinthians 13:8).

Pg 29 "to be rooted and grounded in love? (Ephesians 3:17) to be strengthened by the spirit, to have the indwelling Christ, and to be established in love? (Eph 3:18)

Pg 29 "to know the love of Christ" (Ephesians 3:19)

Pg 29 "God lives in us, and this love is perfected in us." (Jn 4:12)

Pg 29 "speak the truth in love" (Ephesians 4:15)

Pg 29 "...that their hearts may be encouraged being knit together in love and attaining to all riches of the full assurance of understanding, to the knowledge of the mystery of God, both of the Father and of Christ," (Colossians 2:2).

Pg 29 "putting on the breastplate of faith and love" (1 Thessalonians 5:8).

Pg 30 "there is no fear in love" (John 4:12)

Pg 31 "new creatures in Christ" (Galatians 5:17).

Pg 31 , "And why do you look at the speck in your brother's eye but do not consider the plank in your own eye?" (Matthew 7:3)

Pg 32 "Love the lord your God with all your heart" (Matthew 22:37).

CHAPTER FOUR

Pg 36 "These are the things you shall do: Speak each man the truth to his neighbor. Give judgment in your gates for truth, justice and peace." (Zechariah 8:16)

Pg 37 "for such a time as this." (Esther 4:4)

Pg 37 "May God give you the power to accomplish all the good things your prompts you to do. Then the name of the Lord Jesus will be honored because of the way you live ad you will be honored along with Him" (2 Thessalonians 1:11-12)

Pg 38 "having then gifts differing according to the grace that is given to us, let us use them: if prophecy, let us prophecy in proportion to our faith; or ministry, let us use it in our ministering; he who teaches, in teaching; he who exhorts in exhortation; he who gives, with liberality; he who leads, with diligence, he who shows mercy, with cheerfulness." (Romans 12:6-8)

Pg 40 "set your mind on things above, not on things in the earth." (Colossians 3:2)

Pg 40 "For the promise is for you and your children..." (Acts 2:39)

CHAPTER FIVE

Pg 44 "I set my rainbow in the cloud and it shall be for the sign of the covenant between Me and the earth." (Genesis 9:13)

Pg 44 , "I will establish your line forever and make your throne firm through all generations." (Psalm 39:3-4)

Pg 45 "Now to the married I command, yet not I but the Lord: a wife is not to depart from her husband. But even if she does depart, let her remain unmarried or be reconciled to her husband. And a husband is not divorce his wife." (1 Corinthians 7:10-11)

Pg 45 "if the wicked restores the pledge, gives back what he has stolen and walks in the statues of life without committing iniquity, he shall surely live; he shall not die in this life, there is no unpardonable sin for the person who truly repents." (Ezekiel 33:15)

Pg 46 "Because your heart was tender and you humbled yourself before God when you heard His words against this place and against its inhabitants and you humbled yourself before me, and you tore your clothes and wept before Me, I also have heard you, says the Lord." (2 Chronicles 34:27)

Pg 46 "But someone will say, 'you have faith, and I have works.' Show me your faith without your works, and I will show you my faith by my works." (James 2:18)

Pg 46 "Faith without works, is no better than words without deeds." (James 2:15-17)

Pg 46 "Faith can be neither seen nor verified unless it shows itself in works." (James 2:18)

Pg 46 "And be kind to one another, forgiving of one another, even as God in Christ forgave you." (Ephesians 4:32)

CHAPTER SIX

Pg 50 "People were bringing little children to Him in order that He might touch them and the disciples spoke sternly to them. But when Jesus saw this, He was indignant and said to them, "Let the little children come to Me; do not stop them; for it is to such as these that the Kingdom of God belongs. Truly I tell you, whoever does not receive the kingdom of God as a little child will never enter it. And He took them up in His arms, laid His hands on them and blessed them." (Mark 10:13-16)

Pg 50 "If any of you put a stumbling block before one of these little ones who believes is Me, it would be better for you if a great millstone were fastened around your neck and you were drowned in the depth of the sea. Woe to the world because of stumbling blocks! Occasions for stumbling are bound to come but woe to the one by whom the stumbling block comes! (Matthew 17: 6-7)

Pg 51 "When I was a child, I spoke like a child, I thought like a child, I reasoned like a child; when I became an adult, I put an end to childish ways." (1Corinthians 13:11)

Pg 51 "Blessed are the poor in spirt, for theirs is the kingdom of heaven." (Matthew 5:3)

Pg 51 "Blessed are those who mourn, for they shall be comforted." (Matthew 5:4)

Pg 52 "Blessed are the meek, for they shall inherit the earth." (Matthew 5:5)

Pg 52 Blessed are they who hunger and thirst for righteousness for they shall be satisfied." (Matthew 5:6)

Pg 52 Such a one whom God now calls a "saint" (1 Corinthians 1:2)

Pg 53 "Blessed are the merciful, for they shall obtain mercy." (Matthew 5:7)

Pg 53 "He delights in mercy" (Micah 7:18)

Pg 53 "Blessed are the pure of heart, for they shall see God." (Matthew 5:8)

Pg 53 "Evil thoughts and greed, slander and arrogance come from the hearts of men. How can the believer keep his heart pure? By keeping it according to the Word of God." (Psalm 119:9)

Pg 53 "That which proceeds out of man, that is what defiles the man. For from within, out of the heart of men, proceed the evil thoughts, fornications, thefts, murders, adulteries, deed of coveting and wickedness, as well as deceit, sensuality, envy, slander, pride and foolishness. All these things proceed from within the man, and they defile the man." (Mark 7:20-23)

Pg 54 "to conform us to the image and likeness of His Son." (Romans 8:29)

Pg 54 "God looks at the heart." (1 Samuel 6:7)

Pg 54 "washing of regeneration" (Titus 3:5)

Pg 54 "leaning of the conscience." (Hebrews 10:22)

Pg 54 "Blessed are the peacemakers, for they shall be called sons of God." (Matthew 5:11)

Pg 54 "Blessed are those who are persecuted for righteousness' sake, for theirs is the kingdom of heaven." (Matthew 5:12)

Pg 55 "The Word of God is a stumbling block to the ungodly." (1 Peter 2:8)

Pg 55 "that I may know Him and the power of His resurrection, and the fellowship of His sufferings, being conformed to His death." (Philippians 3:10)

Pg 55 "Seeing, they do not perceive..." (Matthew 13:13)

Pg 55 "on giving the paralytic a command to 'arise, take up your bed, and go to your house'" (Mark 2:8)

Pg 55 "Do you still not perceive or understand?" (Mark 8:17)

Pg 55 "You will indeed look, but never perceive." (Acts 28:26)

Pg 56 "the Kingdom is within." Luke 17:21)

Pg 57 "Who of you by worrying can add a single hour to his life? (Matthew 6:27)

Pg 57 "What can a man be given in exchange for His soul? (Matthew 6:27)

Pg 57 "Who is my mother and who are my brothers? (Mark 8:36)

Pg 58 Beatitudes (Matthew 5:3-12)

CHAPTER SEVEN (None)

CHAPTER EIGHT (None)

CHAPTER NINE

Pg 79 "I was in prison and you visited me." (Matthew 25:36)

Pg 80 "Do you have eyes and fail to see? Do you have ears and fail to hear? Then Jesus laid his hands on his eyes again; and he looked intently and his sight was restored, and he saw everything clearly." (Mark 8:18, 25)

Pg 80 "For God alone my soul waits in silence; for my hope is from Him." (Psalm 62:5)

Pg 80 "You are my hiding place and my shield; I hope in your word." (Psalm 119:114)

Pg 80 "I rise before dawn and cry for help; I put my hope in your words." (Psalm 119:147)

Pg 80 "God's Chosen Servant will not break a bruised reed...and in his name the Gentiles will hope." (Matthew 12:19, 21)

CHAPTER TEN

Pg 88 "...as the clay is in the potter's hand, so are you in my hand."(Jeremiah 18:6)

Pg 90 "Your eyes saw my unformed body; all the days ordained for me were written in your book before one of them came to be." (Psalm 139:16)

Pg 91 "Yet I had planted you a noble vine, a seed of highest quality." (Jeremiah 2:21)

CHAPTER ELEVEN

Pg 98 "Thy word is a lamp unto my feet and a light unto my path." (Psalm 119:105)

Pg 99 "or do you not know that your body is the temple of the Holy Spirit which is in you, whom you have from God and you are not your own? For you were bought at a price; therefore, glorify God in your body and in your spirit which are God's." (1 Corinthians 6:19-20)

Pg 99 "You formed my inward part; you knitted me together in my mother's womb. I praise you for I am wonderfully made. Wonderful are your works; my soul knows it very well. My frame was not hidden from you; when I was being made in secret, intricately woven in the depths of the earth. Your eyes saw my unformed substance; in your book were written every one of them, the days that were formed for me, when as yet there were none of them." (Psalm 139:13-16)

Pg 99 "Therefore, you shall lay up these words of mine in your heart and on your hand, and they shall be as frontlets between your eyes. you shall teach them to your children speaking of them when you sit in your house, when you walk by the way, when you lie down and you rise up. And, you shall write them on the doorposts of your house and on your gates, that your days and the days of your children may be multiplied in the land of which the Lord swore to your fathers to give them, like the days of the heavens above the earth." (Deuteronomy 11:18-21)

Pg 102 "...therefore, if anyone is in Christ, he is a new creation; old things have passed away; behold all things are new." (2 Corinthians 5:17)

Pg 102 "Because the promise is for you, for your children." (Acts 2:39)

Pg 102 "Having then gifts differing according to the grace that is given to us, let us use them; if prophecy, let us prophecy in proportion to our faith; or ministry, let us use it in our ministering; he who teaches, in teaching; he who exhorts in exhortation; he who gives, with liberality; he who leads, with diligence; he who shows mercy with cheerfulness." (Romans 12:6-8)

Pg 102 Take this Book of the Law and put it beside the Ark of the Covenant of the Lord you God, that it may be there as a witness against you, for I know your rebellion and your stiff neck. If today, while I am yet alive with you, you have been rebellious against the Lord, then how much more after my death? Gather to me all the elders of your tribes, and your officers, that I may speak these words in their hearing and call heaven and earth to witness against them. For I know that after my death you will become utterly corrupt, and turn aside from the way which I have commanded you. And evil will befall you in the latter days, because you do evil in the sight of the Lord to provoke Him to anger through the work of your hands." (Deuteronomy 31:25-29)

Pg 102 "I will put My law in their minds and write it on their hearts, and I will be their God and they shall be my people." (Jeremiah 31:33)

Pg 103 "For God alone my soul waits in silence, for my hope is from Him." (Psalm 62:5)

Pg 103 "there is no fear in love." (1 John 4:18)

Pg 103 "Restore such a one in a spirit of gentleness." (Galatians 6:1)

Pg 103 "I am the vine, you are the branches; he who abides in Me and I in him bears much fruit; without me, you can do nothing." (John 15:1)

Pg 104 "for such a time as this." (Esther 4:14)

Pg 104 ...derived from Jesus' teaching during the Sermon on the Mount (Matthew 5:1-11)

CHAPTER TWELVE

Pg 110 "My Father's house has many rooms; if that were not so, would I have told you that I am going there to prepare a place for you?" (John 14:2)

Pg 111 The beatitudes (Matthew 15:3-12)

Pg 111 "Truly I say to you, unless you turn and become as little children, you will by no means enter the kingdom of heaven." (Matthew 18:3)

Pg 112 : The thief comes to kill and destroy, but I have come that they may have life and have it more abundantly." (John 10:10)

Pg 112 "You are a new creation in Christ. The old has passed away and the new has come." (1 Corinthians 5:17)

Pg 112 "And this is the judgment" the critical moment...that the light is come into the world and men loved the darkness rather than the light. (John 3:19)

Pg 114 "Take courage, my son; your sins are forgiven" (Matthew 9:2)

Pg 114 "perfect love expels all fear" (John 4:18)

Pg 115 "offered up prayers and petitions with loud cries and tears to the One who could save Him from death." (Hebrews 5:7)

Pg 115 "When my Father sends the Advocate as my representative, the Holy Spirit, He will teach you everything and will remind you of everything I have told you. I am leaving you with a gift—peace of mind and heart. And the peace I give the world cannot give. So don't be troubled or afraid." (John 14:26-27)

Pg 115 "Fear not, for I am with you; Be not dismayed, for I am your God. I will strengthen you, yes I will help you. I will uphold you with My righteous right hand" (Isaiah 41:10)

Pg 116 "So He said 'Come' and when Peter had come down out of the boat, he walked on the water to go to Jesus. But when he saw that the wind was boisterous, he was afraid; and beginning to sink he cried out saying, 'Lord, save me.'" (Matthew 14:29-30)

Pg 116 "O my Lord, I am not eloquent, neither before nor since You have spoken to your servant; but I am slow of speech and slow of tongue. He said, O my Lord, please send by the hand of whomever else you may send." (Exodus 4:10,13)

Pg 116 "Do not fret because of the wicked, do not be envious of wrongdoers, for they will soon fade like the grass and wither like the green herbs. Trust in the Lord and do good for you will live in the land and enjoy security. Take delight in the Lord and He will give you the desires of your heart." (Psalm 37:1-4)

Pg 116 "As iron sharpens iron, so one person sharpens another." (Proverbs 27:17)

Pg 117 "You are of your father the devil, and the desires of the father you want to do. He was a murderer from the beginning and does not stand in the truth, because there is no truth in him. When he speaks a lie he speaks from his own resources for he is a liar and the father of it." (John 8:44)

Pg 117 "Pray without ceasing" (1Thessalonions 5:17)

Pg 117 "For God has not given us a spirit of fear, but of power and of love and of a sound mind." (2 Timothy 1:7)

Pg 117 Yea, though I walk through the valley of the shadow of death, I will fear no evil; for you are with me; Your rod and Your staff, they comfort me." (Psalm 23:4)

Pg 118 "For the wages of sin is death but the gift of God is eternal life in Christ Jesus our Lord." (Romans 6:23)

Pg 121 "In his heart a man plans his course but the Lord establishes his steps." (Proverbs 16.9)

About the Author

Donna Stone is a wife, mother and grandmother, residing in Lakeway, Texas where she nurtures the family and delights in grand-parenting, her journey through life includes a military nursing career highlighted with experiences as a flight nurse, chief nurse and mentor. While in Japan, she and her husband, Mike saw the need and opened a Spouse Abuse Shelter. Counseling and ministry go hand in hand. Both were able to speak to the needs of men and women. In her retirement, she taught parish nursing, implemented the Wesley Nurse ministry and continues to teach Bible studies. Just as the call of God led her eventually to seminary, the culmination of her freedom in Christ was the turning point of her understanding life's challenges and pitfalls. She experienced the trauma of fire and recognized God's grace in dealing with it. Her greatest desire was, and is, to help others do the same. Today Donna is active in her church's Women's Ministry and continues to share God's grace with those who share this chapter of life with her. She holds a Doctorate in Theology, Masters' Degrees in Guidance and Counseling and Healthcare Administration, and a Bachelors in Nursing.

About the Artist | Daryl Howard

After receiving her BFA from Sam Houston State University, Daryl lived and taught art at an overseas school in Tokyo in the 1970's. During this time Howard was introduced to a private collection of 18th and 19th century Ukiyo-e woodcuts. Feeling an immediate connection to the works of art and wanting to learn more about the woodblock print making process, Daryl embarked on an apprenticeship with master printmaker Hodaka Yoshida. By the time she left Japan, Howard had become proficient in the medium, well on her way to perfecting the painstaking demands of carving and printing. Immediately returning to graduate school in 1976 at the University of Texas at Austin, she began her experience with a second medium, mixed media collage.

"The technique of woodblock print making is part of my soul. After over forty-five years of sketching, carving and printing, I am still as excited as I was when I pulled my first print with Hodaka Yoshida in Tokyo. The textural thread within my collage work leads from one image to the next. There is something magical about using the elements of the planet: gold, silver, copper, gemstones and pigments made from soils. These processes have become the way of expressing my world. It involves seeing images through a series of shapes, arranged and colored to represent the essence...the magic...that I experience."

About the Process

Woodblock Printmaking

The technique of woodblock print making dates back to the 2nd century B.C. in China. Japan has enjoyed a long tradition of woodblock print making, with woodcuts first appearing in 1770 A.D. Ms. Howard's technique of woodblock printing is exclusively the traditonal Japanese method which she studied in Tokyo, Japan under Master Hodaka Yoshida. A carved woodblock is created for each color in the print. Watercolor and rice paste are applied with a Japanese brush to the wood. A dampened piece of handmade mulberry "Kizuki" paper is placed on the block and pressed, transferring the color to the paper. Two sides of each piece of paper are exactingly cut at right angles for the registration of the paper to the woodblock. The precise hand-registration of the paper to each block must be repeated many times throughout the

creation of one print. Daryl's signature of 22K gold, silver, or copper leaf is applied last as embellishment to the print. Each print is released in limited editions of 50.

Mixed Media Collage

Daryl begins each collage by creating a metallic leafed background. The entire surface is covered with 22K gold, sterling silver, or copper leaf. Cut and torn papers are used to create shapes within the piece and textured areas are created from earth pigments and applied gemstones. Highlighted areas within the piece are created with overlays of metallic leaf. Recent work reflects a return to her beginnings by utilizing segments of antique Japanese woodblock prints and kimono fabrics within her collage. Daryl's collage process is evolutionary – each piece builds and layers into the next.

Made in the USA
Columbia, SC
18 September 2022